KING'S FUND

REPORT OF A WORKING PARTY ON OSTEOPATHY

CHAIRED BY
RT HON SIR THOMAS BINGHAM

King Edward's Hospital Fund for London

First published by
King Edward's Hospital Fund for London
14 Palace Court
London W2 4HT

Typset by
Discript, London WC2N 4BL

Printed and bound by
Hollen Street Press Ltd, Slough, Berkshire

ISBN 1 85551 071 5

FOREWORD

The present position is that anyone can call himself or herself an osteopath and set up in practice. Of course most practitioners do not do this and many have undergone long and rigorous training.

From the viewpoint of the public, there is a growing interest in, and demand for, the services of osteopaths. There is increasing respect for osteopathy among the medical profession, but most people probably do not know that osteopathy is not regulated in the sense that medicine, dentistry, nursing, pharmacy and physiotherapy all are regulated. Thus the public could be at risk from what are, after all, manipulative techniques of a powerful kind, which can do both harm and good. If this seems surprising, it is worth remembering that no other branch of complementary medicine is regulated, and that medicine itself only became regulated in 1858.

Against this background, the King's Fund appointed us to devise a practical means of achieving regulation for the benefit and protection of patients. It was made clear to us that our recommendations should also reflect the widest possible consensus among osteopaths, and be generally acceptable to the medical profession.

We thought it right to consult not only the osteopathic and medical professions and some of the organisations representing the interests of patients, but also to draw on the experience of a wide cross-section of other statutorily regulated professions. As a result of this process of consultation, we think that our Report offers a fair and practical system of statutory regulation for osteopaths, and one which satisfies all the conditions that Her Majesty's Government has said must be met before legislation can be contemplated.

If, as we hope, our recommendations prove acceptable to Parliament and the draft Bill we have annexed to our Report is eventually enacted, osteopathy will be the first of the professions complementary to medicine to achieve statutory regulation. This, we think, would be a significant development. All osteopaths would in future be regulated by a single statutory governing body rather than belonging, as at present, to a fragmented profession. Patients would benefit from the assurance that osteopaths like most other health care professions will be trained to the same high standard of competence. We must emphasise, however,

iii

that our recommendations seek only to regulate the education, training and professional conduct of osteopaths. They do not provide for osteopaths to practise in the National Health Service.

Not all our recommendations are reflected in the draft Bill annexed to our Report, as many of them are too detailed for inclusion in primary legislation and more readily lend themselves to rules drawn up by the statutory Council, subject to approval by the Privy Council. This will afford the profession considerable flexibility and an appropriate degree of self-determination particularly on future educational policy. Nevertheless, we expect the newly appointed representative Council to take account of our recommendations and use them as a guide when formulating their Rules and Regulations.

We have also tried to deal with the difficult transitional question of initial registration in a way that will protect the public and be fair to people who have already been established in practice.

If our recommendations are to become law, osteopaths must put aside differences and rally to a common purpose, to ensure that the public are provided with the safeguards they rightly expect. Not to succeed in this respect will be seen as the profession failing in its responsibility to the public whom it serves.

WORKING PARTY ON OSTEOPATHY

The Rt Hon Sir Thomas Bingham   (Chairman)[1]

Dr J. Armitstead[2]

Ms A. Ferriman[3]

Mr S. Fielding[4]

Mrs J. B. H. Langer[5]

Professor D. Shaw[6]

Sir Ian Todd[7]

The Lord Walton of Detchant[8]

Mr P. Ediss[9]   )
Dr D. Rothman[10]   )   (Observers, Department of Health)

Mr N. Illingworth[11]   (Secretary)

[(1) A Lord Justice of Appeal: (2) A registered medical practitioner, practising osteopathy and formerly a part-time lecturer at a school of osteopathy: (3) Health Correspondent, *The Observer*. (4) A practising osteopath and Vice-Registrar, General Council and Register of Osteopaths: (5) A practising osteopath and President of the College of Osteopaths, Practitioners Association and Register: (6) Emeritus Professor of Clinical Neurology, University of Newcastle upon Tyne, Chairman, Education Committee, General Medical Council: (7) Immediate past President of the Royal College of Surgeons of England: (8) sometime President of the General Medical Council and lately Warden of Green College, Oxford: (9) Civil servant, (Grade 7), Department of Health: (10) Senior Medical Officer, Department of Health; (11) Retired civil servant.]

TERMS OF REFERENCE

"Having regard to the growing public demand for osteopathic treatment and the increasing support, both professional and political, for early legislation to establish a statutory register to regulate the education, training and practice of osteopathy for the benefit and protection of patients, to consider the scope and content of such legislation, to make recommendations and to report."

CONTENTS

SUMMARY OF CONCLUSIONS
AND RECOMMENDATIONS

I. Both the public and the medical profession have over the years come to recognise osteopathic treatment as a valuable complement to conventional medicine.

Paragraphs 4–10

II. Osteopathic practitioners are at present dispersed among a number of different bodies, many of them with a small number of members and possibly with considerable overlap of membership.

Paragraph 13

III. Standards of education and training among those practising as osteopaths vary very widely. The patient has no guarantee that a man or woman practising as an osteopath is competent to do so.

Paragraph 3

IV. There is at present no single body which governs and regulates the osteopathic profession and thus no body which prescribes or enforces standards across the profession.

Paragraphs 4 and 13

V. After wide consultation we are of opinion that there is a general consensus in favour of a scheme of statutory regulation of the osteopathic profession on the lines we recommend.

Paragraphs 17–19 and 24

VI. The benefits to the general public of a statutory system of control of all practising osteopaths would include:
   (a) an assurance that in future all practitioners will be trained to a high standard of competence;
   (b) a guarantee that appropriate standards of professional conduct will be enforceable by a single statutory governing body;
   (c) the establishment of a suitable mechanism for dealing with complaints from the public concerning the conduct of practitioners; and

1

(d) a guarantee that all practitioners are fully covered by professional indemnity insurance.

We accordingly believe the case for legislation to be made out.

Paragraph 20

VII. The primary objective of any scheme of statutory regulation of the osteopathic profession must be the benefit and protection of patients.

Paragraph 26

VIII. For all practical purposes there is no viable alternative to the establishment of a statutory register of osteopaths open to public inspection and published at regular intervals.

Paragraph 26

IX. A General Osteopathic Council similar to the councils responsible for maintaining registers for other professions should be established by statute. It should be a body corporate with power to appoint Committees, in particular an Education, an Investigating, a Professional Conduct and a Health Committee, to appoint a Registrar and other officers, and to levy fees for the initial registration of osteopaths and for subsequent annual renewals of such registrations.

Paragraph 27

X. The Council should consist of 24 members comprising three different groups, viz:
    (A) 12 representatives of registered osteopaths elected from among themselves;
    (B) 8 members appointed by the Privy Council of whom 7 shall be lay members representing the interests of patients and the general public and one who shall be a registered medical practitioner appointed after consultation with the Standing Conference of Medical Royal Colleges and Their Faculties in the United Kingdom; and
    (C) 4 representatives of schools and institutions providing education and training in osteopathy.

Paragraphs 28-32

XI. In order to allow sufficient time for the Council to arrange for the appointment of Committees and officers, the visitation of schools and institutions and the drawing up of Rules for the registration of osteopaths and for the election of the 12 Group A members the first Group A members should be appointed by the Privy Council and should serve for one term of three years from the day on which legislation comes into force.

Paragraph 29

XII. The Privy Council should ensure that the Group A members appointed by them to serve on the first Council, though not chosen as delegates of particular organisations, should so far as practicable reflect a cross section of good professional opinion and experience.

Paragraph 30

XIII. Arrangements for the election of Group A members drawn up by the first Council, and subject to the approval of the Privy Council, should provide inter alia for:

(a) a minimum of one member to represent osteopaths practising in Scotland;

(b) one to represent osteopaths practising in Wales;

(c) one to represent osteopaths practising in Northern Ireland;

(d) one to be a registered osteopath who is also a registered medical practitioner; and

(e) eight to be elected by registered osteopaths practising in England.

All 12 members elected under these arrangements shall serve for five years and shall be eligible to stand for re-election for further terms of five years.

Paragraphs 29–31

XIV. The Council should decide whether to divide England into constituencies for the purposes of the election. Should they decide not to do so, arrangements should be made to limit the number of elected members resident or practising in Greater London to a maximum of three.

Paragraph 31 (iii)

XV. The Council should have discretion on whether to hold a by-election to fill a vacancy for an elected member occurring in the last year of a five year term.

Paragraph 31 (iv)

XVI. Although Group A members need not reside or practise in the constituency, if any, for which they seek election, the electorate for a constituency should comprise only those registered osteopaths who live or practise in the constituency concerned. Osteopaths who practise in more than one constituency or who live in a different constituency from that in which they practise shall have only one vote and should choose in which constituency they will exercise it.

Paragraph 31(v)

XVII. Group B members should be appointed for a term of five years from the outset and should be eligible for reappointment for further terms of five years.

Paragraph 32

XVIII. The four Group C members shall be nominated, after consultation with such schools of osteopathy as the Council shall approve to award registrable qualifications, by the Education Committee. These members shall serve for a term of five years and shall be eligible for renomination for further terms of five years. Initially, however, the Privy Council, after consultation with the Secretary of State for Education and Science, and the four Health Ministers for the United Kingdom, shall appoint one person experienced in medical education and three osteopaths currently engaged in the education and training of osteopaths to serve as members of the first Council for one term of four years.

Paragraph 33

XIX. The foregoing arrangements are designed to provide opportunities for gradual change of membership, while at the same time ensuring continuity of experience and expertise by staggering terms of office.

Paragraph 34

XX. The first Chairman of the Council shall be one of the 7 lay members appointed by the Privy Council and shall hold office until the first meeting of the Council after the first election of Group A members. At that meeting the Council shall elect a Chairman from among its members to hold office for the duration of his or her term of office as an elected, appointed or nominated member of the Council. The retiring Chairman may be re-elected if he or she is re-elected or reappointed to the Council, so long as his or her term of office as Chairman does not exceed 7 years in total. The Chairman of the Council, save for the first Chairman, may be removed from office by a majority vote of the Council.

Paragraph 35

XXI. All members of the Council shall retire on reaching their 70th birthdays.

Paragraph 36

XXII. The Council may by majority vote resolve that any member who through ill health or otherwise fails to attend four consecutive meetings of the Council shall cease to be a member of the Council.

Paragraph 36

XXIII. There is no case for affording representation to osteopaths practising or resident overseas.

Paragraph 37

XXIV. The Council will need to consider what standards of education and training should be required of new entrants to the profession in order to ensure that patients will be competently and safely treated. These standards should be embodied in an Order approved by the Privy Council.

Paragraph 38

XXV. Initial registration should not be restricted to those practitioners of good character who hold a qualification recognised by the Council as entitling them to automatic registration and who hold or undertake to take out professional indemnity insurance. Practitioners of good character who are able to satisfy the Council that:

(i) they have not been convicted of an offence sufficiently serious as to warrant the Council refusing to admit their names to the Register;

(ii) they have devoted a substantial part of their working time to the safe practice of osteopathy in the United Kingdom for five years in aggregate out of the seven years immediately preceding the day on which legislation first comes into force; and

(iii) they either hold or will take out professional indemnity insurance

shall be entitled to be registered.

Paragraphs 39–40

XXVI. A person of good character practising as an osteopath who does not hold a qualification entitling him or her to be registered automatically and who is unable to satisfy the requirements described in Paragraphs 39 and 40 should nonetheless be afforded the opportunity of applying to the Council for his or her name to be admitted to the Provisional Register. Such applications should be approved where the applicant can show that he or she:

(i) is of good character;

(ii) has not been convicted of an offence sufficiently serious as to warrant the Council refusing to admit his or her name to the Provisional Register;

(iii) has devoted a substantial part of his or her working time to the practice of osteopathy in the United Kingdom for four years in aggregate out of the six years immediately preceding the day on which legislation comes into force and

(iv) undertakes to complete any additional training and pass any examination or test of competence required by the Council within a maximum of five years from the day on which legislation comes into force.

Paragraph 41

XXVII. The Council will be expected, so far as as practicable, to arrange for the continued education of students who had begun but not completed their professional training at a school or institution from which the Council subsequently withdraws approval. Such arrangements might include, for a student in the latter stage or his or her training, entry to the Provisional Register on condition that he or she undertakes such further training and passes such examination or test of competence as the Council may prescribe.

Paragraph 43

XXVIII. The Council's responsibility for oversight of the education, training and practice of osteopaths will include responsibility for determining the future of osteopathic education having regard to:

(i) the changing requirements and responsibilities of clinical practice;

(ii) developments within the European Community; and

(iii) the need for a strong research base.

Paragraph 44

XXIX. The osteopathic members of the Working Party have set out in Appendix D their preliminary views on the minimum levels of osteopathic competence likely to be required for registration in the future.

Paragraph 44 and
Appendix D

XXX. Any person whose initial application for admission to the Register or the Provisional Register is refused will have a right of appeal to the High Court.

Paragraph 45

XXXI. The Council should draw up Rules governing the registration of practitioners practising in this country who trained overseas.

Paragraph 46

XXXII. The Council should be empowered by amendment of Rules to make continued registration conditional on attendance at periodic courses of refresher training. Such amendment of Rules should not be made until similar conditions are introduced for other health care professionals in this country and in any case should not be made without the consent of the Privy Council.

Paragraph 47

XXXIII. Notes for guidance on ethical conduct are preferable to rigid rules of conduct. The Council, who will prepare, review, and, when necessary, up-date such notes, should make it clear that osteopaths registered under the proposed legislation should not take or use the title "doctor" in connection with their clinical practice, unless they are also registered medical practitioners or make it clear to the public that they are not medically qualified.

Paragraph 49

XXXIV. Notes for guidance on ethical conduct should make it clear that unacceptable professional conduct embraces substandard practice and deficient performance.

Paragraph 50

XXXV. In addition to the Education Committee mentioned above the Council should be required to establish:

    (i)   an Investigating Committee responsible for investigating all complaints

7

and allegations of unacceptable professional conduct by registered osteopaths and for deciding whether the evidence supporting such a complaint is prima facie sufficient to warrant the preferment of charges;

Paragraph 52(i)

(ii) a Professional Conduct Committee responsible for the hearing of charges of unacceptable professional conduct against a registered osteopath at the instance of the Investigating Committee and where such charges are found to be proved for imposing appropriate penalties;

Paragraph 52(ii)

and

(iii) a Health Committee responsible for hearing cases referred to it by the Investigating Committee where it seems to the latter that there is prima facie evidence of ill health sufficient to warrant either suspending a practitioner's right to practise altogether or requiring him or her as a condition of continuing registration to comply with certain conditions (e.g. to practise under supervision).

Paragraph 52(iii)

The constitutions and functions of these Committees are described in Appendix C.

XXXVI. The penalties which the Professional Conduct Committee should be empowered to impose (in order of seriousness) should be:
  (i) Admonishment;
  (ii) Imposition of conditions of continuing registration;
  (iii) Imposition of a fine up to level 5 of the Scale of Fines in the criminal courts;
  (iv) Temporary suspension from the Register; and
  (v) Deletion from the Register.

In addition or as an alternative the Committee should have power to order a practitioner against whom there is a finding of unacceptable professional conduct to pay the costs of the hearing.

Paragraph 53

XXXVII. The Health Committee should be empowered:
  (i) to impose conditions of continued registration;
  (ii) to suspend a practitioner's right to practise;

(iii) to extend such suspension, where after a further hearing it seems advisable in the interest of the practitioner or the public to do so; and, exceptionally,

(iv) to delete his or her name from the Register.

Paragraph 54

XXXVIII. It would not be appropriate for the Health Committee to impose financial penalties.

Paragraph 54

XXXIX. The Professional Conduct and Health Committees should have power to redirect cases to each other.

Paragraph 54

XL. A registered osteopath who is aggrieved by a decision of the Professional Conduct or Health Committee should have a right of appeal to the Judicial Committee of the Privy Council.

Paragraph 55

XLI. The Council must appoint a barrister, advocate or solicitor of 10 years standing as legal assessor to the Professional Conduct Committee; and must draw up Rules of procedure for the conduct of proceedings by those Committees. The Rules will be subject to the approval of the Privy Council.

Paragraph 52

XLII. It should be a criminal offence for an unregistered person to take or use the title "Osteopath", "Osteopathic Practitioners" or "Osteopathic Physician" or in any way describe his or her work, with or without qualification, as osteopathy, provided that members of other professions such as chiropractors and physiotherapists, are not prevented from claiming to use or using osteopathic techniques.

Paragraph 60

INTRODUCTION

1. Osteopathy is a system of diagnosis and treatment which lays its main emphasis on the structural and mechanical problems of the body. It is not an alternative to conventional medicine but a complementary discipline which offers patients an additional treatment option for certain conditions which can affect the body's framework. In short osteopaths are concerned with the biomechanics of the body and the maintenance of proper mechanical function. Osteopathic treatment involves the use of predominantly gentle manual methods of treatment and utilises a diagnostic procedure similar to a conventional medical examination but with particular attention to detailed assessment of the patient's musculoskeletal system.

History

2. Osteopathy came to the United Kingdom at the turn of the century, and the profession's largest school, the British School of Osteopathy, was founded in Westminster in 1917.

3. As the law stands, anyone may call him or herself an osteopath and practise as such in the United Kingdom. There is no obligation to undergo formal training of any kind. The courses currently available vary from 4 year full time degree and diploma courses at one extreme to a few weekends' instruction in manipulation at the other. The patient has no guarantee whatsoever that a man or woman holding himself or herself out as a practising osteopath is competent or fit to do so.

4. In 1936 a Bill to regulate the practice of osteopathy was introduced in the House of Lords. Although this Bill was later withdrawn, it led to the majority of practising osteopaths accepting the recommendation of the then Minister of Health to a Select Committee of the House of Lords that the profession should establish a voluntary Register and a Council charged with the responsibility of establishing high standards of osteopathic training, education and practice, and for producing an appropriate code of professional conduct for those on the Register. This became the General Council and Register of Osteopaths (GCRO). There is, however, no legally enforceable obligation on any practising osteopath to register.

Developments since 1980

5. In May 1986 "a kite flying" Osteopaths Bill was laid before the House of Commons under the 10 minute rule. Although it was always known that the Bill could not make further progress it established the existence of a large body of all-party support for a system of statutory regulation for osteopaths.

6. In June 1986 the British Medical Journal published a survey of general practitioners in the Avon area which demonstrated that 93% of doctors in the area thought there should be statutory regulation of practitioners of complementary therapies.

7. A *Which?* report of October 1986 suggested that osteopathy was the most widely used complementary therapy; that the majority of patients who consulted an osteopath did so because of back pain; and that 82% of those patients claimed to have been cured or improved by treatment.

8. It was also evident that the attitude of the medical profession towards osteopathy had changed significantly. The British Medical Association accepted that there was an organised, reputable and coherent body of knowledge underlying osteopathic practice.[1] The British Medical Association is also on record as respecting the education and professional standards which membership of the General Council and Register of Osteopaths entails and believing that the increasingly common instances of cross-referral between general practitioners and osteopaths enhance to the patient's benefit the possibilities of treatment available.

9. In 1988 the Council for National Academic Awards granted degree status to the 4 year diploma course of the British School of Osteopathy.

10. In June 1988 His Royal Highness The Prince of Wales gave a luncheon at Kensington Palace at which Health Ministers and the Presidents of the General Medical Council and the Medical Royal Colleges were present. The latter made it clear that they regarded osteopathy as a profession complementary to medicine and saw no objection to legislation for the statutory regulation of osteopaths being laid before Parliament. The Prince

---

1   Report of speech by the late Dr John Dawson, Under Secretary, BMA, at the University of East Anglia (*Doctor*, September 20th 1984).

of Wales suggested the establishment of a Working Party to examine detailed proposals for such legislation.

11. The Management Committee of the King Edward's Hospital Fund for London (of which The Prince is President) announced in the autumn of 1989 the establishment of a Working Party with the following terms of reference:

> "Having regard to the growing public demand for osteopathic treatment and the increasing support, both professional and political, for early legislation to establish a statutory register to regulate the education, training, and practice of osteopathy for the benefit and protection of patients, to consider the scope and content of such legislation, to make recommendations and to report."

The Working Party's approach to its task

12. We met for the first time as a Working Party on 5th December 1989 and since then have met on 14 other occasions. In the course of our work we have consulted all the main osteopathic bodies in the United Kingdom with a registering function, the principal bodies representative of registered medical practitioners (e.g. the General Medical Council, the Standing Conference of Medical Royal Colleges and Their Faculties and the British Medical Association), the General Dental Council, the United Kingdom Central Council for Nursing, Midwifery and Health Visiting, and the Council for the Professions Supplementary to Medicine, as well as organisations representing patients, consumers and educationalists. A full list of all the bodies consulted will be found at Appendix A. We have also examined closely the different statutes regulating other self-governing professions.

13. We began by circulating a factual questionnaire to those osteopathic bodies with a registering function consulted by the Monopolies and Mergers Commission and listed by them at Appendix 4.1 of their Report on Advertising (Cm 583). The process of consultation reinforced our preliminary views that the profession is fragmented and that practising osteopaths are dispersed among a number of different bodies. Many of these have a small number of members and there is possibly some considerable overlap of membership. (See Table 1 below.)

TABLE 1

Number of Members of Osteopathic Organisations with a Registering Function

(Figures relate to period 1989/1990 and members in some organisations will have increased due to influx of graduates)

Name of Organisation	Number of Members	Number belonging to other organisations
1. British and European Osteopathic Association	84	"Quite a number but no record of these"
2. British Faculty of Osteopaths	100	Not stated
3. British Osteopathic Association	95	50 (Members of GCRO)
4. College of Osteopaths	140	14
5. General Council and Register of Osteopaths	1388	Less than 10 except for 30+ medical members of BOA
6. Guild of Osteopaths	150–200*	Vast majority are members of other organisations
7. International Guild of Natural Medicine Practitioners	–	All members of Guild of Osteopaths. Amalgamated April 1990
8. Natural Therapeutic and Osteopathic Society	78	8
9. Osteopathic and Naturopathic Guild	105	Amalgamated with Guild of Osteopaths April 1991

*As a result of amalgamations with the International Guild of Natural Medicine Practitioners and the Osteopathic and Naturopathic Guild, the Guild of Osteopaths claim to have increased their membership to 300 at the end of April 1991.

Note: The London and Counties Society of Physiologists were also consulted: they do not claim to register osteopaths but said they had between 200 and 250 members who designate themselves "manipulative therapists".

14. Based on the replies to our questionnaire, which we summarise at Appendix B, we estimate that at the beginning of 1990 there were about 2,000 osteopaths in membership of one or more of the bodies which maintain a register and exercise some form of discipline over their members. We were unable to eliminate overlapping membership from our estimates as not all organisations keep records in sufficient detail. No firm figures are available for the number of practitioners providing osteopathic treatment in this country as there is no obligation on practitioners to belong to any of the bodies consulted.

15. Subsequently we circulated for comment in March 1990 provisional proposals which might form the basis of legislation to regulate the education and conduct of osteopaths in the United Kingdom. This consultative letter was favourably received by most recipients, subject in most instances to comments only on points of detail. Having discussed carefully and at length the comments received, and adopted those modifications to our original proposals which seemed to us to have merit, we considered whether we should at once prepare our final report. We were, however, conscious of the importance which successive Government spokesmen have attached to the need for the widest possible consensus about the way forward, and it accordingly seemed to us desirable to afford a further opportunity for comment. We therefore embarked on a second round of consultation in December 1990. We have taken account of the further comments of respondents to this second round of consultations and, where it seemed appropriate to us to do so, have further modified our proposals. We have been very greatly helped by the answers we have received from those consulted, and would wish to acknowledge the time and trouble which have been taken in answering our questions.

The case for legislation

16. Although on more than one occasion Government spokesmen have indicated their support in principle for legislation to regulate the education, training and practice of osteopaths in the United Kingdom, and though our terms of reference assume that the case for legislation has been clearly established, one of the respondents to our first consultative letter questioned some of the assumptions in our terms of reference. It seems to us, therefore, that although our terms of reference only require us to establish the broad principles on which such legislation should be based, it is desirable to outline

the case for legislation in our Report and to incorporate our recommendations in a draft Bill suitable for presentation to Parliament in due course.

17. At present anyone, irrespective of the nature and length of his or her training may take or use the title "osteopath", thus exposing patients unwittingly to the risk of incompetent diagnosis and treatment and reflecting adversely on the reputation of the profession as a whole. Moreover there are wide variations in training standards. We accept that patients should enjoy the maximum freedom of choice. At the same time we agree with a speech by the then Minister for Health in November 1987 in which he stressed the importance of safeguards for the general public. We share his view that such safeguards should include an adequate clinical training for all osteopaths; an ability on their part to recognise (a) conditions where osteopathic treatment is contra-indicated or would be inappropriate and (b) cases where a patient should be referred to a registered medical practitioner; and an assurance of competence to treat patients.

18. Because membership of any of the bodies which claim to maintain a register of osteopaths is purely voluntary such bodies have in practice no effective sanctions enabling them to enforce minimum standards of education, training or competence. Thus, for example, a member of an osteopathic body who has offended against its code of practice and whose name has been struck off may continue to practise unimpeded provided he or she does not claim to be a member of that particular body. Nor can any of the registering bodies prevent the practice of osteopathy by charlatans or inadequately trained osteopaths. This seems to us to be a matter for public concern.

19. Moreover, at a time when the Government is progressively implementing the recommendations of the Monopolies and Mergers Commission that professionals should be free to advertise their services more widely than ever before, most osteopaths consider that liberalisation of restrictions on professional advertising should go hand in hand with statutorily enforceable powers to regulate the education, training, practice and minimum standards of competence of the professionals concerned. In practice such statutory powers are enjoyed by, among others, doctors, dentists, veterinary surgeons, barristers, solicitors, architects, pharmacists, nurses, midwives, health visitors, opticians and the professions supplementary to medicine. Osteopaths, however, although required by the Monopolies and Mergers Commission to bring their practice in relation to professional advertising into line with

those of the professions we have mentioned above, have no statutorily enforceable means of regulating and controlling their members.

20. The benefits to the general public of a statutory system of control of all practising osteopaths would include:
    a) an assurance that in future all practitioners will be trained to a high standard of competence;
    b) a guarantee that appropriate standards of professional conduct will be enforceable by a single statutory governing body;
    c) the establishment of a suitable mechanism for dealing with complaints from the public concerning the conduct of practitioners; and
    d) a guarantee that all practitioners are fully covered by professional indemnity insurance.

Possibility of extending the Professions Supplementary to Medicine Act (the PSM Act) 1960

21. Given that it is to the advantage of practitioners and patients alike that practising osteopaths should be subject to some form of statutory control over their education, training, competence and professional conduct, we considered carefully whether the case for legislation would be sufficiently met by extending the provisions of the PSM Act to include osteopaths. Exploration of this course was urged on us by the British Osteopathic Association, a body which registers medically qualified osteopaths, and it was favoured by the Council for the Professions Supplementary to Medicine (the CPSM). We were unable to accept this proposal, however, because despite the attractions of a solution that in theory should not require recourse to Parliament, we were satisfied that the ability of the CPSM and its professional Boards to regulate professionals other than those working in the NHS or the personal social service departments of local authorities is too limited to enable them effectively to regulate osteopaths, virtually all of whom work wholly in the private sector.

22. In practice a member of one of the professions regulated by the CPSM who is in full time private practice is not legally obliged to maintain his or her registration, since registration is required only for purposes of employment in the National Health Service or the personal social services of local authorities. Moreover an organisation which wishes to train students solely for private practice need not apply for CPSM approval of its courses.

23. It seemed to us therefore that without substantial amendment of the PSM Act, including protection of title for each of the professions covered by that Act, no significant benefits would accrue to the general public or to osteopaths from linking themselves to the CPSM machinery. The BMA also had reservations about the wisdom of this course. In our view, provided the majority of practising osteopaths are agreed on the scope and content of proposed legislation to regulate the education, training and practice of osteopathy, and so long as their proposals are also acceptable to the medical profession, the case for a Bill dealing only with osteopaths would appear to be much stronger than the alternative of attempting to amend the PSM Act. Even if we saw merit in this proposal, we would hesitate to recommend it, since none of the osteopathic bodies we consulted favoured tying the profession to the CPSM machinery and even the British Osteopathic Association did not press the suggestion. It may furthermore be doubted whether some of the professions now subject to the PSM Act 1960 are entirely happy to be so.

Support for our proposals

24. Our enquiries and consultations show that there is a remarkable degree of support among the osteopathic bodies we consulted and the principal associations representative of medical practitioners for the proposals set out below. In our judgement that support is such as to constitute that broad consensus about the best way forward which Government spokesmen have stressed is an essential prerequisite of legislation. We were greatly encouraged by a recent speech of Baroness Hooper who, when speaking for the Government in the House of Lords, expressed the hope that our work would make possible early legislation to secure statutory regulation of the osteopathic profession and that this would be seen as a model and a viable precedent which other professions in the field of complementary medicine might find useful to follow. We also note that in its recent policy document "A fresh start for health" the Labour Party welcomes the progress towards self-regulation within the complementary medicine disciplines. It states its willingness to give this progress legislative backing by introducing national systems of accreditation and registration for those disciplines which have developed high standards of training and practice (among them osteopathy) in order to protect the public against unqualified practitioners.

Possibility of a Bill covering osteopathy and chiropractic

25. Having rejected the idea of what might be termed a PSM solution, we considered the suggestion of a Bill covering chiropractors as well as osteopaths. We know that chiropractors wish to promote legislation to regulate the education and practice of chiropractic in this country and we acknowledge the similarities between chiropractic and osteopathy. While we recognise that a single Bill to regulate both professions is superficially attractive, we are advised that it is doubtful whether this would be practicable at the present time. Moreover, our terms of reference asked us to consider only the position of osteopaths; any extension of our remit would effectively have required us to embark on a further and more extensive round of consultation in the knowledge of Government's clearly expressed preference for legislation dealing with one profession at a time. A simple amalgamation of the two professions would not, we feel sure, be acceptable. In those circumstances we decided not to seek an extension of our remit but to recommend a Bill to regulate only the education, training and practice of osteopaths in the United Kingdom. In the following paragraphs we set out our recommendations for legislation for the statutory regulation of osteopathy in the United Kingdom and our reasons for favouring particular solutions.

Need for a register of osteopaths

26. As we made clear in our consultative letter of 22nd March, 1990 we took as our starting point the two basic assumptions of our terms of reference, first that osteopathy is now publicly and professionally recognised as a professional activity of therapeutic value, and secondly that the benefit and protection of patients must be the primary objective of any scheme of statutory regulation. In considering how best in the interests of patients to regulate the practice of osteopaths we considered whether, as suggested by our terms of reference, a register is a necessary feature of a scheme of statutory regulation. In studying the statutory schemes which govern other professions we noted that each scheme, despite differences of detail, is based on the maintenance of a register. In the light of this we *concluded that for all practical purposes there is no viable alternative to a statutory register of osteopaths which should be open to inspection by members of the public.* None of the organisations that we consulted dissented from this conclusion. Most statutorily regulated professions publish their registers in full at regular

intervals and update them once a year by publishing supplements. *We recommend that the register of osteopaths should be published on a similar basis.*

Need for a General Osteopathic Council

27. Another feature common to the schemes mentioned above is the establishment of a Governing Council of the profession responsible inter alia for maintaining and for prescribing conditions of entry to the Register. The statutes governing other professions generally provide for the Secretary of State or the Privy Council to appoint members of the first Council – usually after consultation with such bodies as appear to them to be representative of members of the profession concerned – and, after the Council has drawn up appropriate electoral arrangements, for a proportion, nowadays usually a majority, of the Council, to be elected by members of the profession whose names are on the Register. We inclined to the view that similar arrangements would be equally appropriate for osteopaths, unless in the course of the consultative process to which we were committed some better scheme were suggested. In practice there was general support for a General Osteopathic Council modelled on similar lines to the councils governing the other professions we had studied. Briefly this Council would be a body corporate charged with responsibility for performing and fully financing the functions assigned to it by statute and entitled to do anything which in its opinion might be calculated to facilitate the proper discharge of those functions. These would include power to appoint a Registrar and other officers, the members of the statutory committees mentioned in paragraphs 33 and 52 and Appendix C below, and such other committees as the Council considers necessary, as well as the right to charge fees for initial registration of an osteopath and the subsequent annual renewal of such registration. Since the establishment of such a Council was generally supported we went on to consider its size and composition. Having regard to legislation governing other professions, the advice so generously given to us by those responsible for the day to day working of those schemes on the problems to be avoided, and the overall size of the osteopathic profession, we favour a Council, neither so large as to be unwieldy, nor so small as to be unrepresentative. In the light of comments received in the course of consultation on our provisional proposals *we recommend that the Council should not exceed 24 members.*

Constitution of a General Osteopathic Council

28. Again following precedents in other legislation, we envisage such a Council comprising three different groups viz:

    Group A   a number of representatives of registered practitioners elected from among themselves;

    Group B   a number of members, predominantly lay persons, to represent the interests of patients and the general public, appointed by the Privy Council; and

    Group C   a number of representatives of schools and institutions providing education and training in osteopathy.

Group A members

29. Again we were fortunate in being able to draw on the advice and expertise of officials of the governing councils of other professions; and hope that as a result our proposals avoid some of the pitfalls which others have encountered. The process of making arrangements for the initial registration of members, the appointment of committees, a Registrar and other officers, the visitation and approval of training schools, the validation and approval of syllabuses and qualifying examinations and the election of Group A members of the Council will, we believe, take much longer than might be supposed. In order to allow sufficient time for the completion of these initial arrangements we *recommend that the first Group A members should be appointed by the Privy Council and serve for a term of three years from the day on which legislation comes into force.*

30. A factor which emerged in the course of our consultations was the concern of the smaller osteopathic organisations that the first Council should not lose sight of their particular interests. Although we understand this concern we are unable to accept the suggestions of some of these bodies that the first Council should consist of one or two representatives of each of the osteopathic organisations. Such an arrangement in our judgement would result in over-representation of the minority and under representation of the majority of practising osteopaths. At the same time we are anxious that the voices of these smaller bodies should be heard. We recommend that the Privy Council *should seek to ensure that the Group A members appointed by them to serve on the first Council, though chosen not as delegates of particular organisations but rather for the knowledge and expertise which as individuals*

they can bring to the work of the Council, should so far as practicable reflect a cross-section of good professional opinion and experience.

31. The Group A members of the first Council will retire at the end of their three year term of office and will be replaced by 12 osteopaths elected by registered osteopaths (including provisionally registered osteopaths) from among themselves in accordance with electoral arrangements drawn up by the first Council and approved by the Privy Council. (The retiring members will of course be able to stand for election.) They will hold office for five years and may offer themselves for re-election for further terms of five years. Although detailed arrangements for the election of Group A members should, we think, be determined by the first Council there are a number of issues which we would expect the Council to take into account. These are:

    (i) Despite the relatively small numbers of osteopaths practising in Scotland, Wales and Northern Ireland we consider it essential for the electoral arrangements to include provision for the election of a minimum of one member to represent osteopaths practising in Wales, one to represent osteopaths practising in Scotland and one for those practising in Northern Ireland. (N.B. Similar provisions are made in legislation governing other self regulating professions.)

    (ii) Similarly, we recommend that one of the 12 Group A members should be a registered osteopath who is also a registered medical practitioner, elected by all registered osteopaths.

    (iii) *The remaining 8 Group A members should, we recommend, be elected by registered osteopaths practising in England.* Whether for this purpose England should be divided into 8 constituencies is a matter which we recommend be determined by the Council. *Whatever the Council decide we recommend that in order to achieve a balanced representation of practising osteopaths not more than three of the 8 Group A members elected by osteopaths resident in England should be resident or practise in the* Greater London area (i.e. the area covered by the former Greater London Council).

    (iv) Bearing in mind the cost of by-elections we considered a suggestion made to us by officials of the governing body of another profession that by-elections should not be held in the first or fifth year of the term of office of elected members. We are of opinion that while it would not be reasonable to disenfranchise a particular area in the first year of a five year term, there are stronger grounds for allowing the Council to decide for itself whether to hold a by-election in the fifth year of a five year term, to fill the vacancy by appointment, or to leave the seat unfilled until the next general election of Group A members. *On balance we recommend that the Council be empowered to exercise discretion on this issue.*

(v) On the general issue of voting arrangements *we recommend that if constituencies are to exist Group A members need not be resident or practise in the constituency for which they seek election or are elected but that the electorate for a constituency should comprise only those registered osteopaths who either live or practise in the constituency concerned; and that where a registered osteopath* either practises in more than one constituency or practises in a different constituency from that in which he or she lives he or she should have only one vote and must therefore choose in which constituency to exercise that vote. Nor should the fact that we have provided for one of the Group A members being also a registered medical practitioner prevent any other registered osteopath who is also medically qualified from standing as a candidate for any of the other 11 Group A seats on the Council.

Group B members

32. The second group of members of the proposed General Council (Group B) would be predominantly laymen appointed by the Privy Council to represent the interests of patients and the general public. Increasingly in recent years Parliament has seen fit to strengthen the lay membership of the governing bodies of statutorily regulated professions. We think it is right that there should be a strong lay element on the proposed General Osteopathic Council to represent the interests of patients and the general public. This is a view impressed upon us by the various consumer organisations that we consulted and is in accord with more recent provisions for other regulatory bodies. Accordingly we *recommend that 7 lay* persons be appointed by the Privy Council to serve on the General Osteopathic Council and to hold office for a term of five years. Such members would be eligible for re-appointment for further terms of five years. In addition to these seven lay members *we recommend that the Privy Council should also appoint, after consultation with the Standing Conference of Medical Royal Colleges and Their Faculties in the United Kingdom, a registered medical practitioner to serve as a member of the General Osteopathic Council for a term of five years.* It seems to us that the Privy Council is the most appropriate body to oversee the activities of a General Osteopathic Council not only because it performs a similar function for a number of other self-governing professions, and has, therefore, greater experience than any other body of

selecting persons of standing to represent the public interest, but also because in practice these powers of the Privy Council are exercised by members of the Government of the day, and the Council is thus indirectly accountable for its actions to Parliament.

Group C members

33. Most governing bodies of statutorily regulated professions include in their membership a number of representatives of universities or training institutions which provide training and award registrable qualifications for the relevant professional discipline. In our view, having regard to the size of the osteopathic profession, *four places on the General Osteopathic Council should be filled on the nomination of the Council's Education Committee after consultation with such schools of osteopathy as the Council shall approve to award registrable qualifications.* [For details of the constitution and functions of the Education Committee see Appendix C.] These four members, who would be eligible to be nominated for further terms of office *would serve for a term of five years.* As, however, the Council and/or its Education Committee will need time in which to visit, inspect and approve training schools and institutions *we recommend that initially the Privy Council, after consultation with the Secretary of State for Education and Science and the four Health Ministers of the United Kingdom, should appoint to serve as members of the Council one person experienced in medical education and three osteopaths currently engaged in the education and training of osteopaths. These four members would serve for one term of four years,* after which they would be replaced by the four members nominated by the Education Committee.

34. The foregoing proposals should, while providing opportunities for gradual change in the membership of the General Council, ensure continuity of experience and expertise by staggering the terms of office of the three groups. It was felt that a Council composed as we have suggested would strike a correct balance between the opinions of professional osteopaths and those of the general public.

Chairman of the Council

35. *We recommend that the first Chairman of the General Osteopathic Council should be one of the lay persons to be appointed by the Privy Council. He or she should hold office for a term of 3 years* (i.e. until the first meeting of the Council after the first election of Group A members). At that meeting the

Council should elect a new Chairman from the membership of the Council. The Chairman elected by the Council, will hold office for the duration of his or her term of office as an elected, or an appointed, member. He may be re-elected as Chairman if he is re-elected or re-appointed to the Council, provided that his term of office as Chairman does not exceed 7 years in total. The Chairman of the Council (save for the first Chairman) may be removed from office on a majority vote of the Council.

Retiring age for Council members

36. *We recommend that all members of the General Council should retire on reaching their 70th birthdays.* This, we note, is laid down for the General Medical Council in the Medical Act, 1983. Although we realise that many individuals over this age are capable of making a meaningful contribution to the counsels of important committees and representative bodies, we think it desirable nevertheless to suggest a maximum retiring age for all members similar to that applicable to members of the governing bodies of other self-regulatory professions. If a Council member fails, through ill-health or otherwise to attend four consecutive meetings, the Council should have power by a majority vote to resolve that such member cease to be a member of the Council and be replaced.

37. Finally under this heading we considered carefully the suggestion of one respondent to our consultative letter that at least one of the Group A members should be elected to represent registered osteopaths practising overseas. We concluded that (quite apart from the practical difficulty for the Council of keeping in touch with osteopaths overseas, many of whom would not maintain their registration) since the Council would have no effective or enforceable jurisdiction outside the United Kingdom *there was no case for affording representation to overseas osteopaths.* An osteopath normally resident overseas who wishes to practise on a regular basis in the United Kingdom, would have to apply for registration and once registered would be eligible to participate in the election of Group A members.

Arrangements for registration

38. If there is to be a Register and a Council then it would be the duty of the Council to maintain that Register and decide on the conditions of entry to it. In our judgement in the medium and longer term no very serious issues of principle are likely to arise. The Council will, however, need to consider

very carefully what standards of education and training should be required of new entrants to the profession in order to ensure so far as is reasonably possible that patients will be competently and safely diagnosed and treated. These standards would then be embodied in an Order which would take effect, as is provided in several similar schemes, only when approved by the Privy Council. Experience has shown that arrangements for registration are better incorporated in Rules made under an Act of Parliament than in the Act itself, since this enables a Council to modify conditions of entry to the register without recourse to amending primary legislation. Such Rules are still subject to the approval of the Privy Council.

Transitional arrangements

39. A more difficult problem concerns the transitional provisions which should govern initial entry to the Register. We take the view that it would be impracticable and unjust to restrict initial registration to those practitioners who hold a qualification recognised by the Council as entitling them to automatic registration and who can fulfil the requirements in sub-para-graphs (a), (b), and (c) below. Practitioners without such a qualification who have practised safely and competently for many years should, we think, also be admitted to the Register automatically, provided they can produce to the General Council:

    (a) evidence of good character
        (which might take the form of submitting the names of two referees);

    (b) an undertaking by the practitioner concerned that he or she has not been convicted of a criminal offence sufficiently serious to warrant the Council refusing to enter his or her name in the Register. If an applicant has a criminal conviction he or she should be required to state what it is;

    (c) evidence that he or she holds professional indemnity insurance or is willing to take out such insurance; and

    (d) evidence of practical experience over a period of years (see paragraph 40 below).

We should make make it clear, with reference to sub-paragraph (b), that offences of a relatively trivial nature, unrelated to professional practice, such as minor motoring offences, would not be treated as a bar to registration. Whether more serious offences, or minor offences committed repeatedly, should be treated as a bar would be a matter for the Council. In exercising its judgement the Council would be concerned to protect members of the public and maintain public confidence in the competence, fitness and reliability of registered and provisionally registered osteopaths.

40. In our consultative letter of 22nd March 1990 we set out two possible options which might form the basis of legislation. The second of these, subject to a number of minor modifications, met with general approval. Accordingly *we recommend that a practitioner applying for full registration who does not hold a qualification recognised by the General Council (in addition to the requirements in paragraph 39 (a), (b), and (c)) be* required to demonstrate to the satisfaction of the General Council that he or she has devoted a substantial part of his or her working time to the safe practice of osteopathy in the United Kingdom for five years in aggregate out of the 7 years immediately preceding the day on which the Act first comes into force.

Provisional Registration

41. A person practising as an osteopath who does not hold a qualification entitling him or her to be registered automatically and who is unable to satisfy the requirements described in paragraph 40 should not be debarred from practising but should be afforded the opportunity of applying to the Council for his or her name to be admitted to *the Provisional Register. Such applications should be approved where the applicant can satisfy the requirements in paragraph 39 (a), (b), and (c) and can demonstrate that he or she has devoted a substantial part of his or her working time to the practice of osteopathy in the United Kingdom for four years in aggregate out of the six years immediately preceding the day on which the Act first comes into force, provided that he or she undertakes to complete any additional training and pass any examination or test of competence required by the Council within a maximum of five years from the said date.*

42. These proposals, it must be emphasised, are designed to facilitate the transition from voluntary to statutory regulation of the whole profession. In our opinion, there should be no continuing need for the proposed system of provisional registration beyond the period of 7 years mentioned in para 41 above. The purpose of provisional registration is to give those osteopaths currently in practice who are unable to satisfy the relatively generous conditions for initial full registration an opportunity, *while continuing to practise osteopathy*, to raise their professional education to the minimum standard considered necessary for full registration (e.g. the equivalent of a

prescribed qualification) without depriving them, meanwhile, of their right to earn a living

43. We would expect the Council to arrange so far as is practicable for the continued education of students who had begun but not completed, before the Act came into force, their professional training at a training school or institution from which the Council subsequently decided to withdraw approval or which closed of its own volition. In such instances we think that where practicable the Council should use its best endeavours to arrange for the students concerned either to complete their training at another approved school or institution or, where the student was in the latter stages of his or her studies, admit him or her to the Provisional Register on condition that he or she undertakes such further training and passes such examination or test of competence as the Council may prescribe. Looking to the longer term, when the need for the Provisional Register has passed, there may be occasions when the Council will need to make special provision for students in training at a school or institution whose educational standards, facilities or examinations fall below the minimum level deemed necessary for the award of a registrable qualification. At one extreme this may result (subject to any direction of the Privy Council) in the closure of a school while at the other some restriction of the numbers of students in training may be all that is needed. In either instance the Council will need to ensure so far as is practicable that suitable alternative arrangements are made for students in training at the time to continue their professional education.

Levels of osteopathic competence

44. Some respondents to our first consultative letter asked us to provide a clear indication of our views on the minimum levels of osteopathic competence required for registration in the future (i.e. after the special arrangements for initial registration have lapsed). We do not feel that this Working Party is qualified to carry out that task. The members of the Working Party with osteopathic qualifications have, however, summarised their preliminary views on this subject and that summary appears at Appendix D. We considered whether to indicate in our report which training qualifications we thought should be recognised by the Council as giving a clear entitlement to registration but were satisfied that we as a Working Party lacked the knowledge, expertise and the time necessary to undertake a detailed appraisal of training schools, courses or qualifying examinations. It will be

for the Council on the advice of the Education Committee to establish minimum levels of competence and safety. The Council's responsibility for oversight of the education, training and practice of osteopaths will include responsibility for determining the future direction of osteopathic education, having regard to

(a) the changing requirements of and responsibilities of clinical practice;

(b) developments within the European Community, and

(c) the need for a strong research base.

Right of Appeal

45. A practitioner whose initial application for admission to the Register or the Provisional Register is refused will have a right of appeal to the High Court.

Secondary Legislation

46. Not all the foregoing provisions need be included in primary legislation: such matters as the precise manner in which applicants for registration are required to produce evidence of their good character, conditions for the approval of training schools and institutions and the validation of training courses and qualifying examinations are in our view better dealt with in Rules made under the relevant legislation, subject to the approval of the Privy Council and, where necessary, Parliament. As indicated in para 38 above, this would facilitate the introduction of changes without recourse to amendment of primary legislation while still maintaining Parliamentary approval of changes. Revised Rules approved by the Privy Council would be incorporated in a Statutory Instrument subject to the negative procedure. Similarly *we recommend that the General Council should draw up a set of Rules governing the registration of practitioners practising in this country but trained overseas.*

Need for post-registration training

47. Initially we were concerned to devise some means of ensuring that registered osteopaths keep themselves up to date by regular attendance at post-registration courses and seminars. In our consultative letter of 22nd March 1990 we invited comments on the suggestion that continuing registration should be made conditional on continuing osteopathic education. This proposal, if adopted, would have empowered the Council to withdraw the registration of practitioners who failed to observe this condition. In the light of reactions

to this idea, we doubt whether it would be viable for some years to come. At present the profession would not, we think, be able to provide the volume of post-registration training and refresher courses sufficient to enable the General Council to make continued registration conditional on regular post-registration training. Furthermore, in the first five years of the Council's existence a substantial part of training effort may have to be devoted to the education and training of osteopaths on the Provisional Register. Even so, we are concerned that once a practitioner has been admitted to the Register, the registering body will have no power to require him or her to update his or her education and knowledge. Although we believe that most professionals do endeavour to keep in touch and familiarise themselves with new developments and techniques, we would like to see periodic refresher training made mandatory on all practising osteopaths. Until, however, such conditions are introduced for other health care professionals in this country we hesitate to recommend that continued registration of osteopaths should be conditional on continued osteopathic education from the date the Act comes into force. Nevertheless, we think there are grounds for empowering the Council to impose such conditions subsequently by amendment of the Rules governing registration, subject to the consent of the Privy Council. *We so recommend.*

Professional conduct

48. One of the primary functions of the Council of a self-regulating profession is to secure a high standard of professional conduct among registered practitioners. Although detailed arrangements for ensuring this vary slightly from one profession to another, the features common to most professions are, first, the promulgation of ethical notes for the guidance of practitioners or rules of professional conduct; secondly, machinery for investigating allegations of unacceptable professional conduct; and thirdly, procedures governing the preferment of charges before, and the hearing of charges and the imposition of penalties by, a suitably constituted domestic tribunal. These procedures are designed to ensure that any practitioner accused of unacceptable professional conduct is fully informed of the complaint against him or her and is afforded a proper opportunity to answer it.

49. We favour the issue of Notes for Guidance on ethical conduct in preference to a code of Rules, because such rules can be undesirably rigid and concentrate attention on the letter rather than the spirit of what constitutes good professional conduct. It will be for the Council to prepare, review and,

when necessary, up-date such Notes. We recommend that in any such Notes it should be made clear that osteopaths registered under the provisions of the proposed legislation should not take or use the title "doctor" in connection with their clinical practice unless they are also registered medical practitioners, or make it clear to the public that they are not medically qualified. In case of doubt practitioners should consult the Council.

50. *It is also our opinion that* Notes for Guidance on ethical conduct should make it clear to practitioners that *"unacceptable professional conduct" should inter alia embrace "substandard practice and deficient performance."* No doubt the Council will also have regard to existing guidance on ethical conduct published by the voluntary registering bodies.

51. Normally, in legislation governing other professions, the initial investigation of a complaint against a practitioner is undertaken by a Preliminary Proceedings or Investigating Committee, whose membership is entirely different from that of the Committee which would hear any charges which the Investigating Committee might formulate. In more recent times, for the better protection of both practitioners and public, statutory provision has been made for the establishment of a Health Committee to deal with those practitioners who should not be allowed to practise for reasons of ill health.

52. *Accordingly we recommend that in addition to appointing the members of the Education Committee mentioned in Paragraph 33 above the General Osteopathic Council should be required to appoint the members of:*
    (i) an *Investigating Committee* responsible for investigating all complaints against or allegations of unacceptable professional conduct by a registered osteopath and for deciding whether the evidence advanced in support of such a complaint is prima facie sufficient to warrant the preferment of charges or cases. (A criminal conviction may without need for further proof be treated as unacceptable professional conduct);
    (ii) a *Professional Conduct Committee*, responsible for the hearing of charges of unacceptable professional conduct preferred against a registered osteopath at the instance of the Investigating Committee and, where such charges are found to be proved, for imposing appropriate penalties; and
    (iii) a *Health Committee* responsible for hearing cases referred to it by the Investigating Committee where it seems to the latter that there is prima facie evidence of ill health sufficient to warrant either suspending a practitioner's right to practise altogether or requiring him or her as a

condition of continuing registration to comply with certain conditions (e.g.: to practise under supervision). The Health Committee would have power after a further hearing to extend a period of suspension in appropriate instances.

Details of the constitution and functions of these Committees are set out at Appendix C. The Council may appoint such other Committees as it thinks necessary for the effective discharge of its duties. We also recommend that the General Council be required to appoint a barrister, advocate or solicitor of at least 10 years standing as Legal Assessor to the Professional Conduct Committee and that Rules for the conduct of proceedings before the Professional Conduct and Health Committees should be drawn up by the Council and approved by the Privy Council.

Range of penalties

53. We have considered carefully the range of penalties which the Professional Conduct Committee might be empowered to impose on practitioners against whom there is a finding of unacceptable professional conduct. We note that the range of penalties available to the Professional Conduct Committees of other professions varies from a single power to strike off the register to a much wider range including a power to fine. Our own preference is for the widest possible range of penalties to enable the Professional Conduct Committee to tailor the penalty to the seriousness of the offence. Accordingly we *recommend that the penalties which the Professional Conduct Committee of the General Osteopathic Council should be empowered to impose (in order of seriousness) should be*
    (i)   admonishment;
    (ii) imposition of conditions of continuing registration (e.g.: practise under supervision; attend refresher training courses);
    (iii) imposition of a fine up to level 5 of the scale of fines in the criminal courts, such fine to be recoverable as a civil debt;
    (iv) temporary suspension from the Register, and
    (v)   deletion from the Register.

In addition or as an alternative to the foregoing *the Committee should have power to order a practitioner against whom there is a finding of unacceptable professional conduct to pay the costs or part of the costs of the hearing in such reasonable sum as the Committee may assess.*

54. *We recommend that the Health Committee should have power:*
    (i)   to impose conditions of continued registration;
    (ii) to suspend a practitioner's right to practise;
    (iii) to extend such suspension, where after a further hearing it seems advisable in the interest of the practitioner or the public so to do; and exceptionally
    (iv) to delete his or her name from the Register.

It would not, in our view, be appropriate for the Health Committee to have power to impose financial penalties. However we think it right that *the Professional Conduct and Health Committees should have power to redirect to* each other cases referred to either of them by the Investigating Committee.

Right of appeal

55. In accordance with the general practice among other statutorily regulated professions *we recommend that any registered osteopath who is aggrieved by a decision of either the Professional Conduct or Health Committee should have the right to appeal to the Judicial Committee of the Privy Council.*

Restriction of title

56. The statutory schemes which we have considered vary widely in the provisions which they make as to the effect of not being registered. In some instances it is provided that anyone who is not registered may not hold himself or herself out as carrying on or in any way carry on the specified professional activity. In other instances an unregistered person is not prohibited from carrying on the activity but is prohibited from using a particular professional title or describing his or her work in a particular way. In either case an unregistered person is not entitled to suggest that he or she is registered. We considered with care which of these two approaches would be the more appropriate for osteopaths: while we were inclined to favour the second approach, before coming to a firm conclusion we sought comments on both approaches in our consultative letter of 22nd March 1990. The second approach was very generally favoured. There was a large measure of support for the need to restrict title, if registration is to be effective and give the public adequate safeguards against unqualified practitioners.

57. It would have been very hard to implement the first approach in a fair and effective manner. There are a number of practitioners in fields closely allied to osteopathy. Having considered the problem ourselves, and having invited comment in our consultative letter, we are satisfied that it would be very difficult (if not impossible) to define osteopathy in such a way as to include that discipline while excluding other related disciplines. At the same time, particularly bearing in mind recent statements by Government spokesmen expressing a preference for legislating for one profession at a time, we concluded that it would neither be feasible nor desirable to attempt to embrace within the statutory scheme we are proposing for osteopaths other professionals practising in closely allied fields.

58. We feel that now, and increasingly in the future if our proposals take effect and become known, it is the terms "osteopath" and "osteopathy" which will be recognised and respected by the public and, importantly, by other professionals as a guarantee of professional competence, conduct and integrity.

59. This approach, if adopted, would mean, for instance, that an unregistered person could carry out manipulative treatments and call himself or herself a manipulative therapist, but could not call himself or herself an osteopath or in any way describe his or her work as osteopathy, even with some qualifying description.

60. Accordingly *we recommend that it should be a criminal offence for an unregistered person to take or use the title "osteopath", "osteopathist", "osteo-therapist", "osteopathic practitioner" or "osteopathic physician" or in any way describe his or her work as "osteopathy", with or without qualification*, provided that members of other professions (e.g.: chiropractors, physiotherapists) should not be prevented from claiming to use osteopathic techniques.

Conclusion

61. In conclusion we commend the foregoing proposals to all practising osteopaths, to the principal medical, educational and other osteopathic organisations whom we have consulted in the course of our deliberations, and to Her Majesty's Government and both Houses of Parliament as a practicable and widely accepted basis for legislation to regulate the education, training and practice of osteopathy in the United Kingdom. So confident are we that legislation on the lines we have recommended would

command wide all-party support, we have presumed to annexe to our Report a draft of a Bill which in due course we hope will be laid before Parliament, ideally with the support of the Government of the day.

T. H. Bingham (Chairman)
J. Armitstead
A. Ferriman
S. Fielding
J. B. H. Langer
D. Shaw
I. Todd
Walton of Detchant
N. Illingworth (Secretary)

November 1991

APPENDIX A

Organisations and individuals consulted or from whom communications were received by the Working Party

Osteopathic Organisations and Individuals

British and European Osteopathic Association
British Faculty of Osteopathy
British Osteopathic Association
The College of Osteopaths Practitioners Association and Register
General Council and Register of Osteopaths
Guild of Osteopaths
London and Counties Society of Physiologists
Natural Therapeutic and Osteopathic Society
Osteopathic and Naturopathic Guild
Dr A. J. S. Walker

The Working Party's questionnaire was also sent to the International Guild of Natural Medicine Practitioners, but was returned by the Post Office. It was subsequently confirmed that members of the International Guild were also members of the Guild of Osteopaths and had amalgamated with the Guild.

Medical Organisations and Individuals

The British Medical Association
The General Medical Council
The Standing Conference of Medical Royal Colleges and their Faculties in the United Kingdom
Mr W. A. Souter FRCSE on behalf of the Council of the Edinburgh College of Surgeons

Statutorily Regulated Bodies

The Council for the Professions Supplementary to Medicine
The General Dental Council

The United Kingdom Central Council for Nursing, Midwifery and Health Visiting

Enquiries on specific points were also made of:

the Architects Registration Council, and the

Royal Pharmaceutical Society of Great Britain.

Professional Organisations

Chartered Society of Physiotherapy

Consumer Organisations

The Association of Community Health Councils

The Consumers' Association

The Patients' Association

Educational Organisations and Individuals

The Council for National Academic Awards

The Committee of Vice-Chancellors and Principals of the

Universities of the United Kingdom

The Department of Education and Science

Sir Norman Lindop, former Principal of the British School of Osteopathy

APPENDIX B

Synopsis of replies to questionnaire sent to osteopathic registering and governing bodies[1]

British and European Osteopathic Association (BEOA)

Membership 84: "quite a number of members who belong to other associations – but no records of these".

Association linked with the Andrew Still College of Osteopathy but accepts graduates of:

    College of Osteopaths;
    London School of Osteopathy;
    British School of Osteopathy;
    Maidstone College of Osteopathy;
    European School of Osteopathy.

Entry may be granted to osteopaths who have graduated from other schools and colleges subject to their satisfying Membership Council as to their competence and the quality of the clinic they practice in (N.B. no details given as to how this assessment or inspection process carried out).

Minimum qualification accepted for membership

Diploma or Degree in Osteopathy from:
1) Andrew Still College of Osteopathy (official teaching body of BEOA).
Also accepts graduates of:
2) London School of Osteopathy associated with Natural Therapeutic and Osteopathic Society (NTOS);
3) British School of Osteopathy   ) Accredited by the General Council
4) European School of Osteopathy   ) and Register of Osteopaths
                                                         (GCRO)
5) Maidstone College of Osteopathy.
6) Sometimes, subject to satisfactory evidence of competence and quality or clinic in which they practice, graduates of other schools.

---

1   Replies received early 1990.

Length and type of training

Andrew Still College of Osteopathy five years Open University.
Contact hours (including clinical training) 1,500.

Examination accredited

Andrew Still College accreditation procedures not stated.

Main functions and activities

Postgraduate training.
Osteopathic undergraduate training.
Membership of a number of osteopathic working parties.
Membership of Parliamentary Lobby for Alternative Medicine.

Codes of conduct/insurance

Code of Ethics.
All members hold professional indemnity insurance.
Complaints are brought to notice of General Secretary who carries out a preliminary enquiry and reports to Executive Council. The Executive Council can then hold an enquiry to which the member will be invited to attend. Council can exonerate, reprimand or expel member.

British Faculty of Osteopathy (BFO)

Membership open to "qualified" osteopaths and those in training. Full membership granted to diplomates after two years full time practice.
Membership approximately 100.

Minimum qualification accepted for membership

Graduates of 4 licensed institutions of BFO (not specified).
Full membership by election after two years full-time practice.

Length and type of training

Would appear to be of 4 years duration but not stated whether whole or part-time.

Contact hours

Not specified.

Examination accredited

Standards, syllabus facilities, teaching and clinical provision of licensed schools "agreed" by Board of Education and Training of BFO.

Main functions and activities

Unincorporated professional association regulates practice of osteopathy as taught by four licensed institutions. Board of Education and Training (BET) licenses institutions for education and training in osteopathy including natural therapeutics.

Codes of conduct/insurance

Members adhere to Code of Ethics and the British Faculty of Osteopathy offers an insurance policy through an advisory agent, if so desired.

British Osteopathic Association (BOA)

Membership 95 (all medically qualified except seven who trained in USA) – at least 50 members also members of the General Council and Register of Osteopaths (GCRO).

Minimum qualification accepted for membership

Graduate of London College of Osteopathic Medicine.

Length and type of training

13 month post-registration training for registered medical practitioners. Students are all medical practitioners who have 6 years relevant postgraduate clinical experience.

Teaching contact hours

900 hours with supervised patient treatment given in school's own clinic.

Accreditation

Course at London College of Osteopathic Medicine accredited by GCRO who provide external examiners for final clinical examinations.

Main functions and activities

Professional association Register of those who practise osteopathy with a full training in both osteopathic methods and orthodox medicine.
To advance interests of practice and its members.

Supports and contributes to Osteopathic Association clinic, Osteopathic Trusts Ltd, GCRO and London College of Osteopathic Medicine.

Publishes annual Directory.

Informs medical profession concerning osteopathic principles and methods.

Provides input to International Federation of Manual Medicine through UK affiliate British Association of Manual Medicine.

Codes of conduct/insurance

Most members subject to rules of General Medical Council.

Constitution of Association includes reference to "... maintain a fitting standard of ethics ..." Ethical rules are not explicit.

There are no rules regarding insurance against actions for professional negligence.

College of Osteopaths Practitioners Association and Register (CO)

Membership 140, of whom no more than 10% are members of other organisations.

Membership is open to graduates of College of Osteopaths and Maidstone College of Osteopathy which are associated with it. Also accept graduates of GCRO accredited schools:

British College of Naturopathy and Osteopathy;

British School of Osteopathy;

European School of Osteopathy.

Minimum qualification accepted for membership

Graduates of:

1) College of Osteopaths   ) Associated Schools
2) Maidstone College of Osteopathy)

3) British College of Naturopathy &)
    Osteopathy   ) 4 year full-time courses accredited
4) British School of Osteopathy   ) by GCRO
5) European School of Osteopathy)

Length and type of training

1) College of Osteopaths six years part-time with thesis
    14–15 weekends per year with private study.

Teaching contact hours

College of Osteopaths: Minimum of 1,000 clinical experience obtained in teaching clinic and in private clinics.
Maidstone College of Osteopathy: No information given.

Examination accredited

College of Osteopaths: final examination Board includes external examiners.
Maidstone College of Osteopathy: not known.

Main function and activities

To ensure that members adhere to ethics, code of conduct and are currently insured: Oversees education trust: Oversees training programme of Maidstone College of Osteopathy: Screens, interviews, examines applicants for membership: Arranges postgraduate seminars: Engages in political activities.

Codes of conduct/insurance

Substantial Code of Ethics. No disciplinary procedures listed in code but Ethical Committee investigates all complaints of breaches of code and has powers to censure, fine or expel members.
Membership conditional on current professional indemnity insurance.

General Council and Register of Osteopaths (GCRO)

Membership 1,388.
Fewer than 40 members belong to other registering bodies and of these the vast majority are registered medical practitioners who are in membership of BOA (see above).
Membership restricted to graduates of one of the accredited four year full-time undergraduate courses or from the thirteen month postgraduate course for registered medical practitioners. In case of a newly accredited course former graduates who have passed individual assessment of safety and competence to practice may apply. Membership includes 54 doctors.

Accredited schools/courses

Minimum qualification accepted for membership
The Diploma or Degree of Osteopathy from:
a) British School of Osteopathy (BSO)
b) European School of Osteopathy (ESO)
c) British College of Naturopathy (BCNO)

d) London College of Osteopathic Medicine (LCOM)

Length and type of training

BSO ESO BCNO Four year full-time
LCOM 13 month postgraduate course for registered medical practitioners
(3 days per week)

Contact hours

BSO 3435   ESO 4324   BCNO 3744 (min.)   LCOM 900

Supervised patient contact hours supervised in school's own clinic

BSO 1404   ESO 1593   BCNO 1100   LCOM 900

Accreditation

Diploma: all examinations are subject to external monitoring by GCRO. New BSc degree course at British School of Osteopathy accredited by Council for National Academic Awards (CNAA). GCRO provide team of trained external examiners to all final clinical examinations.

N.B. In the above 3 full-time courses and 13 month postgraduate course private study is assumed to give students opportunity to use in-house library facilities and to prepare project work.

Main functions and activities

The GCRO is run by a full time salaried staff headed by a professional Secretary and Education Officer.
Accredits schools of osteopathy.
Inspects accredited schools regularly.
Monitors final examinations at accredited schools.
Trains external examiners.
Maintains Register.
Publishes annual Directory and educational Journal.
Maintains and enforces strict code of practice.
Provides telephone and written answering service.
Liaises with Parliament, Government departments and EEC.
Arranges consensus meetings with other main osteopathic registering bodies.
Liaises with the four professional associations of accredited schools.
Operates through a number of Standing Committees consisting of:
1) The Education Committee. Divided into External Examiners' Subcommittee, Competence Exercise Working Party, Postgraduate Committee, Assessment Committee.

2) The Ethics Committee.
3) The Executive Committee.
4) The Finance Committee.
5) The Parliamentary & European Liaison Committee.
6) The Public Relations Committee.
7) The Registration Committee.

Codes of conduct/insurance

Extensive code of practice and disciplinary procedures.

Disciplinary procedures: two tier system of tribunals with powers to hear allegations, to adjudicate and to pass sentence. Sanctions include censure, fines up to 2,000 and expulsion. Complaints from public are subject to careful investigation by the Ethics Committee. Members are required to hold professional indemnity insurance cover as a condition of continued membership.

Guild of Osteopaths (GO)

Membership 150–200.

Full and associate membership open to graduates of the Guild's affiliated school, the Northern Counties School of Osteopathy.

Membership also open to graduates of other training schools recognised by Guild (no details). "External graduates" may be admitted to associate membership or full membership on completion of three or five years full-time practice.

The vast majority of Guild members are also members of other associations.

Minimum qualification accepted for membership

Graduates of:
1) Northern Counties School of Osteopathy;
2) External graduates accepted after 3 years (associate) or 5 years (full membership) part-time practice.

Length and type of training

24 weekend course with monthly weekend tutorial for medical practitioners, nurses, physiotherapists and students of other schools teaching alternative therapies such as remedial massage.

Contact hours

Not specified but in addition to 360 hours attendance at School students required to spend a further 750 hours in home study (no details). No evidence of any clinical training.

43

Examination accredited

Diploma in Osteopathy accredited by Board of Guild of Osteopaths.

Main functions and activities

Holds regular workshops, seminars and social functions and a two day Annual Congress.
Publishes a Directory of members.

Codes of conduct/insurance

Brief Code of Ethics, no details of disciplinary procedures.
Medical indemnity insurance required.
N.B. Amalgamated with (1) International Guild of Natural Medicine Practitioners in April 1990 and (2) Osteopathic and Naturopathic Guild (ONG) in April 1991.

London and Counties Society of Physiologists (LCSP)

Do not claim to register osteopaths but have 200–250 members who choose to designate themselves as "manipulative therapists". Official training establishment: the Northern Institute of Massage offers open learning courses in massage and manipulation. Membership restricted to graduates of Northern Institute of Massage.

Minimum qualification accepted for membership

Graduates of
(1) Northern Institute of Massage. (The Institute does not purport to teach osteopathy but only "manipulative" therapy) and
(2) Applicants who have completed training elsewhere to a similar standard.

Length and type of training

Part-time "open learning" correspondence course. Diploma course in remedial massage (1 & 2 years). Additional 3rd (or 4th) year for Diploma in Manipulative Therapy.

Examination accredited

Certificate in manipulative therapy: College reaccredited every 5 years by Council for Accreditation of Correspondence Courses.

Codes of conduct/insurance

Issues a four paragraph "Code of Ethics" with application for membership form. Disciplinary procedures appear to consist of forfeiture of membership at discretion of Council for any breach of code.

Members are required to hold professional indemnity insurance through a master policy in name of the Society.

Natural Therapeutic and Osteopathic Society (NTOS)

78 members: 10% are members of other associations.

Teaching establishment of which Natural Therapeutic and Osteopathic Society is the governing body is the London School of Osteopathy.

Acceptance of an applicant into membership is decided by interview and the possession of a qualification from an approved school (no details given).

Minimum qualification accepted for membership

Diplomate in Osteopathic Medicine from school recognised by the Society. Official teaching body London School of Osteopathy.

Length and type of training

Five years part-time 18 weekends per year.
16 hours per weekend.
234 hours per year.

Patient contact hours

1,000 hours practical clinical experience either in school clinic or on clinical attachment at private practices.

Examination accredited

Diploma internally validated by Principal, Vice Principal and Education Management Committee.

Main function and activities

To keep register of approved practitioners of osteopathy.
To establish and promote highest possible standard and ethical conduct among practitioners.
To equip, operate and maintain a school of osteopathy.
To provide practitioners with facilities for postgraduate training, research and discussion of professional matters and provide external validation committee.

To prepare, print and publish reports, periodicals, books, leaflets and advertisements.

To hold and take part in exhibitions, lectures and conferences.

To encourage and promote co-operation and contact relating to professional matters between members and other professional bodies and between student and practising osteopaths.

Codes of conduct/insurance

Code of Ethics. Disciplinary procedures conducted by Appeals & Disciplinary Committee. Sanctions: caution, admonishment, suspension up to 12 months and removal from the register.

Osteopathic & Naturopathic Guild (ONG)

(Note: This Association amalgamated with Guild of Osteopaths in April 1991.) Membership 105. (Sister organisations run by same Board of Directors are Registers of Herbalists and Homoeopaths.) Offers correspondence courses in herbal medicine, homoeopathy, naturopathy and osteopathy. Membership appears to be restricted to graduates of above courses. All members are expected to be in full time practice within two years of acceptance onto register.

APPENDIX C

Constitution and functions of committees

The Education Committee

1. The General Council shall appoint an Education Committee constituted as follows:

The Chairman of the General Council.

Six members appointed by the General Council from among Group A members.

All 4 Group C members of the General Council.

Three members appointed by the General Council from among Group B members.

In addition the Education Committee with the approval of the General Council may co-opt for a term of not more than 3 years at a time 4 members, being members of the teaching staff of osteopathic training schools or institutions other than those at which Group C members of the Council are employed.

No member of the Education Committee who regularly teaches or lectures at a particular training school or institution may be appointed as a visitor at that school.

The Committee shall elect its own Chairman, but the Chairman of the Council shall not be eligible for election as Chairman of the Committee.

The quorum of the Committee shall be 7, the majority of whom must also be members of the General Council.

2. The General Council shall refer to the Education Committee for advice on *all* matters relating to osteopathic education, training and examinations and in particular the qualifications entitling a person to be registered.

3. The General Council may appoint persons to visit, subject to any directions which the Privy Council may deem it expedient to give and to compliance with any conditions specified in those directions, schools, institutions and other places where instruction leading to a registerable qualification is given to students of osteopathy, osteopaths whose names are entered in the Provisional Register and registered osteopaths following post graduate courses in osteopathy.

4. It shall be the duty of such visitors to report to the Education Committee and the General Council as to the sufficiency of the instruction and the facilities provided in the places which they visit and as to any other matters relating to the instruction which may be specified by the Council either generally or in any particular case; but no visitor shall interfere with the giving of any instruction.

5. On the receipt of a report of a visitation the General Council shall send a copy to the governing body of the training school or institution concerned affording to it an opportunity of making to the General Council within such period as the General Council may specify (not being less than one month) observations on the report or objections thereto.

6. As soon as practicable after the expiration of the period specified under paragraph 5 above the Council shall send a copy of any such report together with any observations thereon or objections thereto together with the Council's comments on the report and on any such observations and objections to the Privy Council.

7. The Council shall have power to remunerate members of the Council as well as non-members for acting as visitors at such rates as the Privy Council may approve.

8. Where it appears to the Education Committee and General Council that the course of study and examinations leading to a registrable qualification in osteopathy are not such as to secure the possession by the graduates of the requisite knowledge and skill for the efficient practice of osteopathy the General Council may make representations to that effect to the Privy

48

Council and on any such representation the Privy Council may, if they think fit, order that any degree or diploma in osteopathy granted by the training school or institution shall not confer any right to be registered.

9. The foregoing powers may be exercised in respect of a specifically described degree or diploma in osteopathy granted by a university, polytechnic, training school or institution. Where such an order is made by the Privy Council no person shall be entitled to be registered in respect of such degree or diploma granted after the time mentioned in the order.

10. The Privy Council may revoke such an order where they are satisfied on further representation from the General Council or otherwise that the governing body of the training school or institution concerned has improved to the satisfaction of the General Council the course of study and examinations, but such revocation shall not entitle a person registered in respect of a degree or diploma in osteopathy granted before the revocation. Any order of the Privy Council under this paragraph may be made conditionally or unconditionally and may contain such terms and directions as appear to the Privy Council to be just.

11. If it appears to the General Council that a training school or institution has attempted to impose on any student an obligation to adopt or to refrain from adopting the practice of any particular theory of osteopathy as a test or condition of admitting him or her to examination or of granting a degree or diploma in osteopathy, the General Council may make a representation to that effect to the Privy Council. On any such representation the Privy Council may direct the governing body of the training school or institution concerned to desist from attempting to impose any such obligation. If the governing body does not comply with the direction the Privy Council may order that the governing body concerned shall cease to have power to grant degrees or diplomas in osteopathy.

The Investigating Committee

1. The Investigating Committee shall consist of not fewer than 8 members of the Council of whom at least 2 shall be lay members and at least 1 shall (if practicable) be a registered medical practitioner. These members may co-opt up to 8 additional members, provided that each co-option shall be

for a term of not more than 3 years at a time and shall be subject to the approval of the Council.

2. The Investigating Committee shall investigate individual cases under paragraphs 3 and 5 below in groups of not fewer than 3 members of whom at least 1 shall be a lay member and (in the case of an investigation under paragraph 5) 1 shall (if practicable) be a registered medical practitioner.

3. An Investigating Committee sub-group shall investigate any complaint, allegation or report of unacceptable professional conduct by any registered or provisionally registered osteopath. For that purpose it shall
    (1) seek to obtain full details of the complaint, allegation or report;
    (2) seek to ascertain what, if any, evidence exists to corroborate or contradict the complaint, allegation or report;
    (3) inform the registered or provisionally registered member of the complaint, allegation or report and invite his or her observations.

4. The Investigating Committee sub-group shall consider the information, evidence and observations which it has obtained under paragraph 3 above and shall consider whether an allegation of unacceptable professional conduct should be laid against the registered or provisionally registered osteopath and, if so, what the substance of the allegation should be. If it considers that the case does merit proceedings before the Professional Conduct Committee it shall refer the case to the full Investigating Committee with a brief summary of its reasons for doing so. Conviction of a criminal offence shall be treated as evidence of unacceptable professional conduct. If the sub-group decides that an allegation of unacceptable professional conduct should not be laid that decision and the brief reasons for it should be at once communicated to the registered or provisionally registered osteopath and to the Committee's informant, if any.

5. An Investigating Committee sub-group shall also consider any complaint, allegation or report that any registered or provisionally registered osteopath is by reason of any impairment of his physical or mental condition unfit to perform his or her professional duties as an osteopath. For that purpose it shall carry out the duties specified in paragraph 3(1)(2) and (3) above.

6. The Investigating Committee sub-group shall consider the information, evidence and observations which it has obtained under paragraph 5 above and shall consider whether in all the circumstances the case merits formal

enquiry by the Health Committee. If it considers that the case does merit formal enquiry it shall refer the case to the Investigating Committee with a brief summary of its reasons for doing so. If it considers that the case does not merit formal enquiry it shall so resolve and shall inform the registered or provisionally registered osteopath accordingly.

7. If, in the course of considering a case under paragraphs 3 and 4 an Investigating Committee sub-group consider that the case would more appropriately be considered under paragraphs 5 and 6 it may so decide and may treat the case as falling under those paragraphs. If, in the course of considering a case under paragraphs 5 and 6 an Investigating Committee sub-group consider that the case would more appropriately be considered under paragraphs 3 and 4 it may so decide and may treat the case as falling under those paragraphs. No decision of the Committee or a sub-group thereof shall be invalidated by the absence of a member who is a registered medical practitioner.

8. Where an Investigating Committee sub-group refer a case to the Investigating Committee under paragraph 4 or paragraph 6 above the Investigating Committee shall consider the case and decide whether it should be referred to the Professional Conduct Committee or the Health Committee, as the case may be, and shall direct accordingly. Notice of such decision shall be given to the registered or provisionally registered osteopath in question. For purposes of carrying out its duties under this paragraph the Investigating Committee may, at the discretion of the Chairman, either meet or act on consideration of the relevant papers by individual members of the Investigating Committee.

9. The Investigating Committee may act where there is a quorum of 7 members, a majority of whom must also be members of the General Council. It shall act on a majority of those present and voting. If there is an equality of votes the Chairman of the meeting at which the vote is taken shall have a casting vote in addition to his vote as a member. The Committee shall not hold oral hearings. There shall be no appeal against the Committee's decisions. Save as specified herein the Committee may regulate its own procedure.

The Professional Conduct Committee

1. The Professional Conduct Committee shall consist of not fewer than 6 members of the Council of whom at least 2 shall be lay members. These 6 members may co-opt up to 4 additional members, provided that each co-option shall be for a term of not more than 3 years at a time and shall be subject to the approval of the Council.

2. Upon the Investigating Committee deciding that a charge of unacceptable professional conduct should be laid against a registered or provisionally registered osteopath, it shall be the responsibility of the Professional Conduct Committee to determine whether the charge is established and, if so, what penalty (if any) should be imposed within the range prescribed in paragraph 53 of this report.

3. The Professional Conduct Committee shall conduct its proceedings in accordance with rules which shall be drawn up and approved by the Council and which will become binding upon approval by the Privy Council. The Professional Conduct Committee may regulate its own procedure insofar as the same is not governed by these rules but shall at all times ensure that the registered or provisionally registered osteopath against whom the charge is laid is fully informed of the case against him and is given a fair opportunity to meet it and to make submissions to the Professional Conduct Committee in mitigation of sentence.

4. The Professional Conduct Committee shall hear charges against registered or provisionally registered osteopaths in public (save to the extent that the interests of any patient or informant shall, in the opinion of the Committee, require any part of any hearing to be conducted privately) and shall announce its decision in public. Such decision shall, if adverse to the registered or provisionally registered osteopath or (at his or her request) if favourable to him or her, be published in an annual report.

5. A registered or provisionally registered osteopath who is aggrieved by the Professional Conduct Committee's decision that a charge is established or by any penalty it imposes shall have a right of appeal to the Judicial Committee of the Privy Council.

6. The Professional Conduct Committee may act where there is a quorum of

5 members, a majority of whom shall be members of the Council. It shall act on a majority of those present and voting. If there is an equality of votes the Chairman of the meeting at which the vote is taken shall have a casting vote in addition to his vote as a member. The Committee shall hold an oral hearing in any case where it considers such a hearing to be necessary or the registered or provisionally registered osteopath requests it. At any such hearing the registered or provisionally registered osteopath shall be entitled to be legally represented.

The Health Committee

1.   The Health Committee shall consist of not fewer than 6 members of the Council of whom at least 2 shall be lay members and at least 1 shall be a registered medical practitioner. These 6 members may co-opt up to 4 additional members, provided that each co-option shall be for a term of not more than 3 years at a time and shall be subject to the approval of the Council.

2.   All references by the Investigating Committee to the Health Committee shall first be considered by a sub-group of not less than 3 members of the Health Committee, one of whom shall be a registered medical practitioner. The sub-group shall have power to seek medical opinions, to invite the practitioner concerned to submit to medical examination and to ask whether he or she is willing to accept the medical examiner's recommendations. Only where the practitioner concerned refuses to submit to medical examination or to accept the medical examiner's recommendations shall the case be referred formally to the Health Committee. In such cases the Health Committee shall enquire whether the registered or provisionally registered osteopath whose case is so referred is by reason of any impairment of his physical or mental condition unfit, whether temporarily or permanently, to perform his or her professional duties as an osteopath.

3.   For purposes of such enquiry the Registrar shall lay before the Committee such materials as were before the Investigating Committee and the Investigating Committee's reasons for making the reference. The Health Committee may obtain such other evidence and opinions (including medical opinions) as it shall consider necessary to make a decision but it shall not

reach a decision without giving the registered or provisionally registered osteopath (or his or her legal representatives)

(1) a summary of the material before the Health Committee (omitting, where appropriate, the name of any informant);

(2) a full opportunity to question adverse witnesses on whom the Health Committee may rely;

(3) a full opportunity to present his or her case, whatever it may be, and to call witnesses.

4. If the Health Committee concludes that the registered or provisionally registered osteopath is not unfit as aforesaid it shall so inform him or her and shall take no further action.

5. If the Health Committee concludes that the registered or provisionally registered osteopath is unfit as aforesaid it shall so inform him or her and shall thereupon consider whether, for the protection of the public and the maintenance of public confidence in the competence, fitness and reliability of registered and provisionally registered osteopaths, the registered or provisionally registered osteopath should

(a) be suspended from practice as an osteopath, and if so whether indefinitely or for what period; or

(b) be permitted to practise only subject to conditions, and if so whether indefinitely or for what period and subject to what conditions;

and may order accordingly.

But the Health Committee may not make any order under paras 5(a) or 5(b) unless or until it has

(a) informed the registered or provisionally registered osteopath (or his or her legal representatives) of the Committee's finding of unfitness;

(b) invited his/her observations and submissions on (a) and (b) above;

(c) offered him or her an opportunity to present evidence or call witnesses relevant to (a) and (b) above;

(d) considered what is the minimum period of suspension or conditional registration and, as the case may be, what are the least burdensome conditions reasonably necessary to satisfy the objects specified above.

Where the Health Committee resolves to suspend a practitioner's right to practise the suspension shall take effect immediately.

6. Notwithstanding any period of suspension or conditional registration imposed by the Health Committee under paragraph 5 above, the Committee may at any time before the expiry of such period either on its own motion or on application duly made revoke such order either forthwith or from such future date as it may specify if of opinion that the continuation of the order is no longer reasonably necessary to satisfy the objects specified above, it being clear at all times that the purpose of the Health Committee's orders is not to penalise the registered or provisionally registered osteopath but to safeguard the public.

7. If, when the period of any order of suspension or conditional registration has expired or is about to expire the Health Committee is of opinion that the impairment which led to the making of the order, or a similar or related impairment, continues and that the objects specified above reasonably require a continuation of the order, whether in the same or in a modified form, it may so order. But the Health Committee may not make an order under this paragraph unless or until it has
    (a) informed the registered or provisionally registered osteopath (or his or her legal representatives) that continuation of the order, whether in the same or a modified form is under consideration;
    (b) invited his or her observations;
    (c) offered him or her an opportunity to present evidence or call witnesses;
    (d) considered what is the minimum period of further suspension or conditional registration and, as the case may be, what are the least burdensome conditions reasonably necessary to satisfy the objects specified above.

    Orders under this paragraph may be repeated as often as the Health Committee consider them to be justified.

8. The Health Committee may act where there is a quorum of 5 members, the majority of whom must also be members of the General Council. It shall act on a majority of those present and voting. If there is an equality of votes the Chairman of the meeting at which the vote is taken shall have a casting vote in addition to his vote as a member. A registered or provisionally registered osteopath who is aggrieved by any decision of the Committee may appeal to the Judicial Committee of the Privy Council. Save as specified herein the Committee may regulate its own procedure.

9. In the case of a provisionally registered osteopath the limit of 5 years

specified in paragraph 41 of this report shall take effect whether or not he or she is for any part of that period or on its expiry subject to any order of suspension or conditional registration made by the Health Committee.

The Committee shall hold an oral hearing in any case where it considers such a hearing to be necessary or the registered or provisionally registered osteopath requests it. At any such hearing the registered or provisionally registered osteopath shall be entitled to be legally represented.

APPENDIX D

Minimum levels of osteopathic competence required for registration

1. The fundamental minimum prerequisites of competent osteopathic practice set out below are based on a paper prepared at our request by the osteopathic members of the Working Party.

2. In order to apply manual therapeutic techniques safely and competently a practitioner must have a sound knowledge of anatomy, physiology, pathology, biomechanics, osteopathic principles and basic medical therapeutics. A practitioner must have acquired sufficient depth of knowledge of the principles of medicine and the pathological processes of underlying disease and be aware of the physiological basis of osteopathic treatment and current concepts regarding the neurobiological mechanisms of manipulative therapy.

3. A practitioner must be capable of taking and interpreting a pertinent case history which should include information about the patient's present complaint including predisposing, precipitating and maintaining factors as well as information about the patient's medical, psychological, social and family history.

4. A practitioner must be able to conduct and interpret an appropriate clinical examination which will include:
   (a) an examination and evaluation of the biomechanics of the patient and a reasoned assessment of the fundamental biomechanical interrelationships within the body's structure.
   (b) the use and interpretation of appropriate and currently acceptable clinical testing procedures and auxiliary investigations, including a clinical examination of the nervous system.

5. A practitioner must be trained to make an appropriate differential diagnosis based upon current knowledge. This should include an awareness that pain associated with certain visceral diseases can mimic pains originating from within the musculoskeletal system. It is essential therefore that a practitioner

should be able to distinguish between pain of a biomechanical nature and that of visceral origin as well as determine whether a pain is derived from the site where it is experienced or referred from another part.

6. A practitioner must be trained to record systematically all relevant information and findings and be able to communicate these, and their relevance, to the patient's general practitioner and/or other health care practitioner.

7. A practitioner must also be aware of the absolute and relative contra-indications to osteopathic/manipulative treatment. The practitioner must be aware of his/her limits of competence and be able to recognise when the patient is suffering from a condition where osteopathic treatment may be inappropriate and which accordingly requires referral to a registered medical practitioner.

8. On completion of an initial examination, the practitioner should be in a position to determine whether osteopathic treatment is appropriate, and if so formulate an appropriate treatment plan and prognosis. The practitioner should be able to communicate his or her findings, diagnosis, prognosis (and possible prophylaxis) to the patient in such a way that the patient's own expectations are taken into consideration.

9. Osteopathic treatment embraces a wide range of manual therapeutic techniques which involve the application of accurately and specifically directed forces to the structures of the body. Practitioners should be familiar with the wide range of osteopathic techniques and know how to apply and modify them appropriately to the patient's particular condition.

10. Practitioners should be aware of the hazards of inappropriate and "over" treatment, and be capable of evaluating, assessing and reassessing the patient's changing condition and any other ongoing therapeutic procedure which the patient may be receiving.

11. To sum up, the practice of osteopathy requires a depth of medical and biomechanical knowledge with a repertoire and refinement of technical skills which short undergraduate or postgraduate courses alone cannot adequately hope to provide. In order to absorb the professional skills and ethical values essential for safe and competent practice all student osteopaths require a continuity of clinical experience combined with substantive interaction with professional lecturers, clinicians and peers in an environment which allows for a synthesis of theoretical learning and practical experience.

OSTEOPATHS BILL

Osteopaths Bill

ARRANGEMENT OF CLAUSES

SCHEDULE:—

BILL

TO

Establish a body to be known as the General Osteopathic Council with the functions of promoting and regulating the practice of the profession of osteopathy; and for connected purposes.

BE IT ENACTED by the Queen's most Excellent Majesty, by and with the advice and consent of the Lords Spiritual and Temporal, and Commons, in this present Parliament assembled, and by the authority of the same, as follows:—

A.D. 1991.

The General Council

5   1.—(1) There shall be a body corporate to be known as the General Osteopathic Council (in this Act referred to as "the General Council") which shall have the general function of developing, promoting and regulating the profession of osteopathy in the interests of the public

10   and the other functions given to them by this Act.

(2) There shall be four committees of the Council, to be known as the Education Committee, the Investigating Committee, the Professional Conduct Committee and the Health Committee, which shall have the functions given to them respectively by this Act.

15   (3) The General Council may appoint such other committees as they consider appropriate in connection with the performance of their functions.

(4) The Schedule to this Act shall have effect with respect to the constitution of the General Council and the Committees mentioned in

20   subsection (2) and their affairs.

Constitution and functions of the General Osteopathic Council and its Committees.

Professional education

2.—(1) The Education Committee shall have the general function of promoting high standards of education in osteopathy and co-ordinating all stages of such education.

25   (2) The General Council shall refer to the Education Committee on all matters relating to such education.

General functions of the Education Committee.

Information to be given by institutions granting qualifications in osteopathy.

3. Every educational institution under whose direction any course of study is taken or by which any examinations are held for the purpose of granting any qualification in osteopathy shall from time to time when required by the General Council give them such information as the General Council may require— 5

    (a) as to the course of study or examinations to be gone through in order to obtain a qualification in osteopathy, and

    (b) generally as to the conditions laid down for obtaining such a qualification.

Powers to appoint visitors.

4.—(1) The Education Committee may appoint any person to visit 10 places in the United Kingdom where any instruction is given to students of osteopathy or registered osteopaths (other than places at which that person regularly gives instruction himself).

(2) Such visits shall be made in accordance with any directions given by the Privy Council with respect to them and shall be subject 15 to any conditions specified in those directions.

(3) It shall be the duty of visitors appointed under subsection (1) to report to the Education Committee—

    (a) as to the adequacy of the instruction given and the facilities provided in the places they visit, and 20

    (b) as to such other matters relating to the instruction as may be specified by the Committee either generally or in any particular case.

(4) On the receipt of any report of a visitor under subsection (3) the Education Committee shall send a copy of the report to the 25 institution under whose direction the instruction is given, and on receipt of that copy that institution may, within such period of not less than one month as the Committee specified at the time they sent the copy of the report, make observations on the report or objections to it. 30

(5) After the expiry of the period mentioned in subsection (4) the Education Committee shall send a copy of the report and of any duly made observations or objections to the Privy Council.

(6) The General Council may remunerate any persons appointed to act as visitors under this section (including their own members) at 35 such rates as the Privy Council may approve.

Recognition of standards and qualifications.

5.—(1) The General Council shall from time to time determine the standard of proficiency which is required by a person for the competent and safe practice of osteopathy and may represent to the Privy Council that it is expedient that that standard should be 40 recognised for the purposes of this Act.

(2) If it appears to the General Council that the standard of proficiency required from persons taking any course of study under the direction of, or examinations held by, any educational institution in the United Kingdom for the purpose of granting any qualification in 45 osteopathy does or will conform to the standard mentioned in subsection (1), the General Council may represent to the Privy

Council that it is expedient that that qualification should be a recognised qualification for the purposes of this Act.

(3) If it appears to the General Council, after consultation with the Education Committee, that the standard of proficiency required from
5 persons taking any such course of study or examinations for the purpose of granting any qualification which is for the time being a recognised qualification for the purposes of this Act does not or will not conform to the standard mentioned in subsection (1), the General Council may represent to the Privy Council that it is expedient that
10 that qualification should cease to be a recognised qualification for the purposes of this Act.

(4) Her Majesty may by Order in Council give effect to any representations made to the Privy Council under this section.

(5) Such an Order under this section—
15 (a) shall not be made unless the Privy Council have considered—

(i) any report made under section 4 which relates to the course, examinations or institution in question and any observations on or objections to any such report of which a copy has been sent to them under subsection (5) of that
20 section, and

(ii) in the case of an Order made by virtue of subsection (3), any representations or objections made to them by the educational institution in question;

(b) shall specify the date as respects the granting of qualifications
25 on and after which it has effect (which may be a date earlier than that on which this Act comes into force);

(c) may be conditional or unconditional; and

(d) may contain such other terms and such directions as appear to the Privy Council to be just.

30 (6) The General Council may by rules make such supplementary provision as they consider necessary in connection with the recognition of standards and qualifications under this section.

(7) In this Act "recognised qualification" means a qualification for the time being specified in an Order made under this section.

35 *Registration*

6.—(1) The General Council shall appoint a registrar (in this Act referred to as "the Registrar") who shall establish and maintain a register (in this Act referred to as "the register") of the osteopaths who are entitled to be fully or provisionally registered under this Act.

Keeping and publication of register of osteopaths.

40 (2) The Registrar shall perform such duties in connection with the register as the General Council may direct, and in the execution of his duties he shall act on such evidence as appears to him to be sufficent in each case.

(3) Any person appointed as the Registar shall hold office for such
45 period and upon such other terms as the General Council may determine.

(4) A certificate purporting to be a certificate under the hand of the Registrar stating that any person is or is not, or was or was not at any date, duly registered in the register shall be prima facie evidence in all courts of law of the facts stated in the certificate.

(5) The General Council shall secure that at least once every three 5 years a correct copy of the register is printed, published and made available for sale (whether in the form of a fresh copy of the whole register or of a supplement to a copy previously printed under this section), and any such copy shall be admissible in evidence (except as respects any honours or distinctions accorded to a registered person).　10

Entitlement to registration.

7.—(1) Subject to the following provisions of this Act, a person shall be entitled to be registered in the register with full registration if he satisfies the Registrar—

(a) either—

(i) that he holds a recognised qualification, or　　　　15

(ii) that in the full qualifying period the periods during which he has spent a substantial part of his working time in the safe and competent practice of osteopathy in the United Kingdom total in aggregate not less than five years;

(b) that he is of good character; and　　　　　　　　20

(c) that he is or, if he is not in practice as an osteopath at the time of his application for registration, he will when he begins or resumes practising be adequately insured against claims made against him for negligence in his practice.

(2) Subject to the following provisions of this Act, a person shall be 25 entitled to be registered in the register with provisional registration if he satisfies the Registrar—

(a) either—

(i) that in the provisional qualifying period the periods during which he has spent a substantial part of his working 30 time in the safe and competent practice of osteopathy in the United Kingdom total in aggregate not less than four years; or

(ii) that on the date on which this Act came into force he was undergoing a course of study or examinations held 35 by an educational institution in the United Kingdom for the purpose of granting a qualification in osteopathy which has been but has ceased to be a recognised qualification;

(b) that he is of good character; and

(c) that he is or, if he is not in practice as an osteopath at the 40 time of his application for registration, he will when he begins or resumes practising be adequately insured against claims made against him for negligence in his practice.

(3) A person may only be provisionally registered under subsection (2) if he undertakes that he will within the period of five years 45 beginning with the date on which this Act comes into force complete such further training and pass such test of his competence as an osteopath as the General Council may require; and—

(a) if the Registrar is satisfied that he has fulfilled his undertaking within that period, he shall be entitled to be registered in the register with full registration; but

5   (b) if the Registrar is not so satisfied, his registration shall lapse at the expiry of that period.

(4) For the purposes of this section the Registrar may require an applicant to furnish him with such references, undertakings or other evidence as the General Council may from time to time direct or, in respect of any matter as to which no such direction is given, as he 10 may think fit.

(5) If, during the period of five years beginning with the day on which this Act comes into force, the Registrar determines that he is not satisfied that a person making his first application for full registration or his first application for provisional registration is 15 entitled to be so registered, the applicant may, within twenty-eight days of being notified of the decision, appeal to the High Court against it.

(6) In this section—

"the full qualifying period" means the period of seven years 20   ending with the day preceding that on which this Act comes into force;

"the provisional qualifying period" means the period of six years ending with that day.

(7) The General Council may by rules make provision enabling 25 persons who have qualified as osteopaths in a place outside the United Kingdom to be registered under this section where the Registrar is satisfied—

(a) that their qualifications are of a standard broadly similar to that of the qualifications recognised under this Act; and

30   (b) that the conditions mentioned in subsection (1)(b) and (c) are satisfied in relation to them.

(8) A person shall be regarded as having a recognised qualification for the purposes of this section if—

(a) he is a national of a member State of the European Commu- 35   nities; and

(b) he has a professional qualification, obtained in a member State other than the United Kingdom, which the Secretary of State has by order designated as having Community equivalence for the purposes of registration under this Act.

40   (9) In subsection (8) "national", in relation to a member State of the European Communities, means the same as it does for the purposes of the Community Treaties.

8.—(1) The General Council may by rules make such provision as they consider appropriate concerning registration under this Act.   Rules with respect to registration.

45   (2) Such rules may in particular make provision as to—

(a) the form and keeping of the register;

(b) the making, periodic renewal, erasure and restoration of entries in it and the charging of fees in respect of those matters;

(c) the form and manner of making applications for registration and the documents and other evidence which must 5 accompany such applications;

(d) the issue of certificates of registration;

(e) the procedure to be followed in the event of an appeal against a refusal of registration under section 7;

(f) the imposition of conditions on registration (including in 10 particular conditions requiring registered osteopaths to undergo further education and training).

Supervision of professional conduct

Guidance on professional conduct and ethics.

9. The General Council may from time to time issue such guidance and advice for members of the profession of osteopathy as it may 15 consider appropriate regarding standards of professional conduct and ethics.

Preliminary investigation of complaints against osteopaths.

10.—(1) Where an allegation is made to the Investigating Committee that a registered osteopath—

(a) has been convicted in the United Kingdom of a criminal 20 offence or has been convicted elsewhere of an offence which, if committed in England or Wales, would constitute a criminal offence (in either case whether before or after registration), or

(b) is guilty of unacceptable professional conduct, or 25

(c) is by reason of his mental or physical condition unfit to perform his professional functions as an osteopath,

the Committee shall investigate the allegation with a view to deciding whether the case ought to be referred for further inquiry—

(i) in the cases mentioned in paragraphs (a) and (b), by the Pro- 30 fessional Conduct Committee, or

(ii) in the case mentioned in paragraph (c), by the Health Committee.

(2) For the purposes of their investigation under subsection (1) the Investigating Committee shall, so far as possible— 35

(a) obtain full details concerning the substance of the allegation;

(b) ascertain what evidence exists to corroborate or contradict the allegation;

(c) in the case mentioned in subsection (1)(b), inform the registered osteopath in question of the allegation and invite 40 him to make observations about it to them within a specified period;

(d) consider any such details, evidence and observations and whether they justify the making of a further inquiry by the Professional Conduct Committee or the Health Committee. 45

(3) If the Investigating Committee decide to refer a case concerning a registered osteopath to the Professional Conduct Committee, they

shall determine the specific terms of the complaint to be referred and inform him of it at the time of the reference.

(4) If the Investigating Committee decide to refer a case to the Health Committee, they shall refer the case with a summary of the 5 reasons for the reference.

(5) If, after investigating an allegation regarding a registered osteopath, the Investigating Committee decide not to refer the case to the Professional Conduct Committee or the Health Committee, they shall inform him and any other person who gave the Committee 10 information relevant to the allegation of that decision, giving them their reasons for it.

(6) There shall be no appeal against a decision of the Investigating Committee under this section.

(7) If at any time during the investigation of a reference to the 15 Professional Conduct Committee or the Health Committee it appears to that Committee that the case in question should have been referred instead to the other Committee, they shall refer the case immediately to that other Committee who shall proceed with the reference as if the case had been referred to them directly by the Investigating 20 Committee originally.

11.—(1) Where the Investigating Committee refer a case concerning any registered osteopath to the Professional Conduct Committee that Committee shall determine whether he has been convicted as is mentioned in section 10(1)(a) or, as the case may be, he is guilty of 25 unacceptable professional conduct.

References to the Professional Conduct Committee.

(2) If the Professional Conduct Committee determine that a registered osteopath has been convicted as there mentioned or is guilty of unacceptable professional conduct, they may—

    (a) admonish him,

30   (b) order that his name be erased from the register from such date as may be specified in the order;

    (c) order that his registration as an osteopath shall be suspended during such period as may be so specified;

    (d) order that his registration shall during such period as may be 35   so specified be subject to such conditions as may be so specified; or

    (e) order him to pay to the General Council a sum not exceeding level 5 on the standard scale for fines imposed on summary conviction of criminal offences.

40   (3) Instead of taking such action as is mentioned in subsection (2) or in addition to taking such action, the Professional Conduct Committee may order a person in respect of whom they have made such a determination as there mentioned to pay such reasonable amount as the Committee assess as the costs of the hearing of his case.

45   (4) A sum ordered to be paid under subsection (2)(e) or (3) may be recovered as if it were a civil debt.

(5) The Professional Conduct Committee—

(a) shall hold an oral hearing if the osteopath whose case is being considered requests it;

(b) may hold such a hearing in any case where they consider it to be necessary before making any determination or order under this section; and

(c) shall hold any such hearing in public (unless in the opinion of the Committee the interests of any patient or other person require any part of the hearing to be conducted in private);

and at any such hearing the osteopath whose case is being considered is entitled to be legally represented.

(6) The Professional Conduct Committee shall secure that any osteopath whose case is being considered by them under this section—

(a) is given full details of any allegation made against him;

(b) is given a fair opportunity to make representations with respect to it and, if the Committee make such a determination as is mentioned in subsection (2) in respect of him, with respect to the action which may be taken against him under this section.

(7) The Professional Conduct Committee shall announce their decision on each case in public and shall secure the publication in an annual report—

(a) of all such determinations as are mentioned in subsection (2) they have made in the year in question; and

(b) if the person in respect of whom the determination was made requests it, of any determination they have made to the contrary.

(8) The General Council shall appoint a barrister, advocate or solicitor of at least ten years standing to act as legal assessor to the Professional Conduct Committee and advise them on questions of law arising in proceedings before them under this section; and the Lord Chancellor or, in Scotland, the Lord Advocate may make rules concerning the functions of such assessors.

(9) A person may be appointed as an assessor under subsection (8) to advise the Professional Conduct Committee generally or for any particular proceedings; and a person so appointed shall hold office in accordance with the terms of the instrument under which he is appointed and may be paid such remuneration by the General Council as they may determine.

References to the Health Committee.

12.—(1) Where the Investigating Committee refer a case concerning any registered osteopath to the Health Committee, that Committee shall determine whether he is by reason of his physical or mental condition unfit to perform his professional functions as an osteopath.

(2) Before making that determination, the Health Committee—

(a) shall consider the information and evidence considered by the Investigating Committee and their reasons for referring the case;

(b) may obtain such other evidence and opinions (including medical opinions) as they consider appropriate;

(c) shall give the registered osteopath whose condition is being considered—

(i) a summary of the evidence they are considering (omitting anything which in their opinion may lead to the identification of any person by whom the original allegation concerning him was made); and

(ii) an opportunity to question any witness on whose evidence the Health Committee may rely, to present a case to the Committee and to call witnesses.

(3) Where the Health Committee determine that the registered osteopath whose condition they have considered is not unfit as mentioned in subsection (1), they shall—

(a) inform him of their determination; and

(b) take no further action.

(4) Where the Health Committee determine that the registered osteopath whose condition they have considered is unfit as mentioned in subsection (1), they shall—

(a) consider whether for the protection of the public and the maintenance of public confidence in the profession, his registration as an osteopath should be suspended for a period (not exceeding one year) or be made conditional, and, if so, whether indefinitely or for a fixed period, and the conditions, if any, to which his registration should be subject;

(b) inform him of their determination of his unfitness and the action, if any, they consider appropriate; and

(c) either—

(i) take no action, or

(ii) subject to subsection (5), order his registration to be suspended or made conditional accordingly.

(5) Before making an order under subsection (4)(c)(ii), the Health Committee shall—

(a) invite the person in respect of whom they propose to make the order to make observations;

(b) give him an opportunity to present evidence and call witnesses concerning their proposals; and

(c) consider what is the minimum period of suspension or, as the case may be, conditional registration and, in the case of conditional registration, the least onerous conditions which may reasonably be imposed to achieve the purposes mentioned in subsection (4)(a).

(6) Where the Health Committee have made an order under subsection (4)(c)(ii), if at any time it appears to them of their own motion or on an application made to them in that behalf that the continuation of the order is no longer necessary to achieve the purposes mentioned in subsection (4)(a), they may by order revoke the order under subsection (4)(c)(ii) either with immediate effect or with effect from such future date as they may specify in the revoking order.

(7) Where—

(a) an order under subsection (4)(c)(ii) has expired or is about to expire, and

(b) it appears to the Health Committee—

    (i) that the person in respect of whom the order was 5 made continues to suffer from the condition which led to the making of the order or a similar or related condition, and

    (ii) that the continuation of the order (whether in the same form or with modification) is still necessary to 10 achieve the purposes mentioned in subsection (4)(a),

they may, subject to subsection (8), order that it continue accordingly.

(8) Before making an order under subsection (7) in respect of any person the Health Committee shall—

(a) inform him that they are considering the continuation of the 15 order under subsection (4)(c)(ii);

(b) invite him to make observations;

(c) give him an opportunity to present evidence and call witnesses concerning their proposals; and

(d) consider what is the minimum period of further suspension or, 20 as the case may be, conditional registration and, in the case of conditional registration, the least onerous conditions which may reasonably be imposed to achieve the purposes mentioned in subsection (4)(a);

and subsection (7) and the previous provisions of this subsection apply 25 to an order continued by virtue of an order under subsection (7) as they apply to an order under subsection (4)(c)(ii).

(9) The Health Committee—

(a) may hold an oral hearing in any case where they consider such a hearing to be necessary before making a determination 30 under subsection (1) or deciding what action to take under subsection (4) or (7) in respect of any person, and

(b) shall hold such a hearing before doing so if that person requests it;

and at any such hearing that person is entitled to be legally repre- 35 sented.

<table>
<tr><td>Appeals from the Professional Conduct and Health Committees.</td><td>

13.—(1) Any person who is or was formerly a registered osteopath and is aggrieved by a decision made in respect of him by the Professional Conduct or the Health Committee may, within 28 days of being notified of the decision, appeal to Her Majesty in Council. 40

(2) No appeal shall lie from a decision of the Health Committee except on a question of law.</td></tr>
<tr><td>Procedure on appeals under s. 13.</td><td>

14.—(1) An appeal to Her Majesty in Council under section 13 shall be made in accordance with this section and such rules as Her Majesty in Council may by Order provide for the purpose of 45 regulating such an appeal.</td></tr>
</table>

(2) The Judicial Committee Act 1833 shall apply in relation to the Professional Conduct Committee and the Health Committee as it applies to a court falling within section 3 of that Act (appeals to Her Majesty in Council to be referred to the Judicial Committee of the Privy Council).

1833 c. 41.

(3) Without prejudice to that Act, on an appeal under section 13 the Judicial Committee may in their report recommend to Her Majesty in Council—

(a) that the appeal be dismissed; or

(b) that the appeal be allowed and the determination or order appealed against be quashed and either—

(i) such other determination or order as the Professional Conduct Committee or, as the case may be, the Health Committee could have made be substituted for the determination or order appealed against; or

(ii) the case be remitted to the Professional Conduct Committee or the Health Committee to dispose of the case under section 11 or 12 in accordance with the directions of the Judicial Committee.

(4) The General Council may appear as respondent on any appeal under this section; and for the purposes of enabling directions to be given as to the costs of any such appeal the General Council shall be deemed to be a party to it whether or not they appear.

15.—(1) Where a person's name has been erased from the register in pursuance of an order under section 11, except in a case where the order is quashed on appeal his name may only be restored to the register if, on an application to the General Council in that behalf, they so direct.

Restoration to the register after erasure under s. 11.

(2) Applications under this section—

(a) shall be made in accordance with rules under section 8; and

(a) shall be referred to the Professional Conduct Committee for determination by them.

16. The General Council shall make rules as to—

Rules as to procedure in disciplinary cases etc.

(a) the procedure of and evidence before the Investigating Committee, the Professional Conduct Committee and the Health Committee and the reference of cases to and transfer of cases between those Committees;

(b) notification of decisions by those Committees;

(c) the formalities to be observed in connection with the making and the effect of the orders and decisions of those Committees; and

(d) such other matters relating to those Committees and their orders and decisions as appear to the General Council to be necessary or desirable.

**Use of names
and descriptions.**

17.—(1) Subject to subsection (2), if any person who is not a registered osteopath—

   (a) describes himself as an osteopath, osteopathic practitioner, osteopathic physician, osteopathist or osteotherapist;

   (b) describes any activity undertaken by him as osteopathy; or   5

   (c) describes himself or any activity undertaken by him in a way likely to suggest that he is an osteopath or practises osteopathy,

whether or not he qualifies that description in any way, he shall be guilty of an offence.   10

(2) A person who is guilty of an offence under subsection (1) shall be liable on summary conviction to a fine not exceeding level 5 on the standard scale.

Miscellaneous and supplementary

**Default powers
of Privy Council.**

18.—(1) If at any time it appears to the Privy Council that the 15 General Council or any of the Committees mentioned in section 1(2) have failed to perform any function conferred on them by or under this Act which should be performed, they may notify the General Council or, as the case may be, the Committee in question accordingly and may give them such directions as they consider appropriate.   20

(2) If the General Council or any of those Committees fail to comply with any directions given to them under subsection (1), the Privy Council may themselves give effect to those directions and for that purpose—

   (a) they may do anything authorised to be done by the General 25 Council or, as the case may be, the Committee in question, and

   (b) they may of their own motion do anything which under this Act they are authorised to do in response to an action as to which there has been such a failure.   30

Interpretation.

19. In this Act—

"the General Council" means the General Osteopathic Council;

"recognised qualification" has the meaning given in section 5(7);

"the register" and "the Registrar" have the meanings given in section 6;   35

"registered osteopath" means a person for the time being registered in the register with full or provisional registration (other than a person whose registration is suspended).

**General
provisions as to
rules made by
the General
Council.**

20.—(1) Rules made by the General Council under section 5(6), 7(7), 8 or 16 or paragraph 11 of Schedule 1 shall not come into force 40 until approved by order of the Privy Council.

(2) Rules made by the General Council under this Act may make different provision for different cases.

21.—(1) Any power of the Privy Council to make orders under this Act shall be exercisable by statutory instrument.

(2) Except as provided in subsection (3), any statutory instrument containing an Order in Council or order of the Privy Council under this Act shall be subject to annulment in pursuance of a resolution of either House of Parliament.

(3) Subsection (2) does not apply to an order approving rules under section 8.

(4) The powers conferred on the Privy Council by this Act shall be exercisable by two or more members of the Privy Council.

22.—(1) This Act may be cited as the Osteopaths Act 1991.

(2) This Act shall come into force on such day as the Secretary of State may by order made by statutory instrument appoint and different days may be so appointed for different purposes and for different provisions.

(3) This Act extends to Northern Ireland.

SCHEDULE

CONSTITUTION OF THE GENERAL COUNCIL AND THEIR COMMITTEES

PART I

THE GENERAL COUNCIL   5

Membership

1.—(1) The General Council shall consist of 24 members.

(2) During the initial three year period twelve members shall be osteopaths nominated by the Privy Council, after consultation with organisations appearing to them to be representative of practising 10 osteopaths; and after that period twelve members shall be persons who have been elected by registered osteopaths from among themselves.

(3) Seven members shall be persons who are not registered osteopaths and are appointed by the Privy Council.

(4) During the initial four year period four members shall be 15 persons nominated by the Privy Council, after consultation with the Secretary of State, of whom—

(a) one shall be a person appearing to the Privy Council to be experienced in the provision of medical education; and

(b) three shall be persons appearing to them to be engaged in the 20 education or training of osteopaths; and

after that period four members shall be persons nominated by the Education Committee, after consultation with the educational institutions by which recognised qualifications may be awarded.

(5) One member shall be a person who is not a registered osteopath 25 but is a registered medical practitioner and is nominated by the Privy Council, after consultation with the body known as the Standing Conference of Medical Royal Colleges and Their Faculties in the United Kingdom or, if that body ceases to exist, such other body as appears to the Privy Council to be appropriate for the purposes of this 30 sub-paragraph.

(6) A person shall not be eligible for membership of the General Council if he has attained the age of seventy.

Election, appointment and nomination of members

2.—(1) At the end of the last day of the period of five years 35 beginning immediately after the initial three year period, and at the end of each successive period of five years, all the elected members holding office as such shall retire together, and elections shall be held accordingly before the end of each of those periods.

(2) An election shall be held to fill a casual vacancy among the 40 elected members if a vacancy occurs more than 12 months before the beginning of the next five-year period, but need not be held if a vacancy occurs within 12 months before such a period.

(3) Of the 12 elected members—

   (a) eight shall be elected by the registered osteopaths whose addresses in the register are in England;

   (b) one shall be elected by the registered osteopaths whose addresses in the register are in Scotland;

   (c) one shall be elected by the registered osteopaths whose addresses in the register are in Wales;

   (d) one shall be elected by the registered osteopaths whose addresses in the register are in Northern Ireland; and

   (e) one shall be a registered medical practitioner elected by registered osteopaths whose addresses in the register are in the United Kingdom (who are eligible to vote for him irrespective of the part of the United Kingdom in which their addresses in the register are situated).

(4) Subject to the previous provisions of this paragraph, elections of members shall be conducted in accordance with an electoral scheme prepared by the General Council and approved by order of the Privy Council.

(5) An electoral scheme under sub-paragraph (4) may be amended in accordance with amendments so prepared and approved.

3. At the end of the last day of the period of five years beginning with the day on which this Act comes into force, and at the end of each successive period of five years, all the appointed members holding office as such shall retire together, and appointments shall be made accordingly before the end of each of those periods.

4. At the end of the last day of the initial four year period, and at the end of each successive period of five years, all the nominated members holding office as such shall retire together, and nominations shall be made accordingly before the end of each of those periods.

Chairman

5.—(1) The Privy Council shall appoint one of the members of the General Council nominated under paragraph 1(3) to be the chairman of the General Council.

(2) Subject to paragraph 8, he shall hold office as chairman until a chairman is elected under sub-paragraph (3).

(3) After the expiry of the initial three year period the members of the General Council shall elect a chairman from among the persons who are for the time being members of it.

(4) Subject to sub-paragraph (5) and paragraphs 7 and 8, the chairman shall hold office as such as long as he holds office as a member of the General Council.

(5) No person may hold office as chairman for more than seven years consecutively.

General provisions as to office as member or chairman

6. A person shall not be disqualified from being a member or the chairman of the General Council by reason of having previously been a member or, as the case may be, chairman.

7. A member and any chairman of the General Council (other than 5 the chairman for the initial three year period) may be removed from office as such by a majority decision of the General Council.

8. A member or the chairman of the General Council may resign from his office as such at any time.

General powers of the General Council 10

9.—(1) Subject to the following provisions of this Schedule the General Council may do anything which is in their opinion calculated to facilitate the proper discharge of their functions.

(2) The General Council may, in particular, pay to their members such fees and such travelling, subsistence or other allowances as the 15 Privy Council may approve.

(3) The powers of the General Council and of any of their committees may be exercised regardless of any vacancy.

(4) No proceedings of the General Council or of any of their committees shall be invalidated by any defect in the election, appoint- 20 ment or nomination of a member or of the chairman.

10.—(1) The General Council may, after paying their expenses, including the payments authorised to be made under paragraph 9 and the salaries, remuneration and other expenses of their officers, allocate any money received by them (whether by fees or otherwise) 25 to purposes connected with education, training or research in connection with osteopathy or any other public purposes in connection with the profession of osteopathy in such manner as they may think fit.

(2) The General Council shall keep proper accounts of all sums 30 received and paid by them and shall arrange for the accounts to be audited.

11.—(1) Except in so far as provision is made by this Act, the General Council may make rules—

(a) for regulating their proceedings; 35

(b) for delegating their functions to committees (including the Committees referred to in section 1(2));

(c) for appointing the members and regulating the proceedings of any committees (other than the Committees referred to in section 1(2)). 40

(2) Nothing in this paragraph shall authorise the General Council to delegate any power of making rules under this Act.

Interpretation

12. In this Part of this Schedule—

"the initial three year period" means the period of three years beginning with the day on which this Act comes into force; and

"the initial four year period" means the period of four years beginning with that day.

PART II

THE COMMITTEES OF THE GENERAL COUNCIL

The Education Committee

13.—(1) The Education Committee shall consist of—

(a) the chairman of the General Council;

(b) the members of the General Council referred to in paragraph 1(4);

(c) nine members appointed by the General Council from among its members, of whom six shall be such members as are referred to in paragraph 1(2) and three such members as are referred to in paragraph 1(3) or 1(5); and

(d) not more than four such other persons as may from time to time be members by virtue of paragraph 17.

(2) At any meeting of the Education Committee such member of the Committee as the Committee shall choose (other than the chairman of the General Council) shall be chairman.

(3) All acts of the Education Committee shall be decided by a majority of the members present and voting, but in the event of an equality of votes, the chairman shall have an additional casting vote.

(4) The quorum for a meeting of the Education Committee shall be seven members of whom at least four shall be members of the General Council.

(5) The Education Committee may appoint a sub-committee to perform any of their functions.

(6) Except in so far as provision is made by this paragraph, the Education Committee may regulate their own procedure.

The Investigating Committee

14.—(1) The Investigating Committee shall consist of—

(a) not less than eight members appointed by the General Council from among its members, of whom at least two shall be such members as are referred to in paragraph 1(3) and, if practicable, one shall be a registered medical practitioner; and

(b) not more than eight such other persons as may from time to time be members by virtue of paragraph 17.

(2) At any meeting of the Investigating Committee such member of the Committee as the Committee shall choose (other than the chairman

of the General Council) shall be chairman.

(3) All acts of the Investigating Committee shall be decided by a majority of the members present and voting, but in the event of an equality of votes, the chairman shall have an additional casting vote.

(4) The quorum for a meeting of the Investigating Committee shall 5 be seven members of whom at least four shall be members of the General Council.

(5) Subject to sub-paragraph (6), the Investigating Committee may appoint a sub-committee to perform any of their functions, and—

    (a) a sub-committee to whom functions under section 10 regarding 10 unacceptable professional conduct are delegated shall consist of at least three members and one shall be a person who is not a registered osteopath, and

    (b) a sub-committee to whom functions under that section regarding physical or mental impairment are delegated must 15 consist of at least three members of whom, if practicable, one shall be a registered medical practitioner.

(6) A decision of a sub-committee of the Investigating Committee to refer a case for further inquiry to the Professional Conduct Committee or the Health Committee must be confirmed by the Inves- 20 tigating Committee itself.

(7) No decision of the Investigating Committee or such a sub-committee as is mentioned in sub-paragraph (5)(b) shall be invalidated by the absence of a member who is a registered medical practitioner.

(8) The Investigating Committee shall not hold oral hearings as part 25 of their investigation of any case.

(9) Except in so far as provision is made by rules under section 16 or by this paragraph, the Investigating Committee may regulate their own procedure.

The Professional Conduct Committee 30

15.—(1) The Professional Conduct Committee shall consist of—

    (a) not less than six members appointed by the General Council from among its members, of whom at least two shall be such members as are referred to in paragraph 1(3) and, if practicable, one shall be a registered medical practitioner; and 35

    (b) not more than four such other persons as may from time to time be members by virtue of paragraph 17.

(2) At any meeting of the Professional Conduct Committee if the Chairman of the General Council is present he shall be Chairman and otherwise such member of the Committee as the Committee shall 40 choose shall be chairman.

(3) All acts of the Professional Conduct Committee shall be decided by a majority of the members present and voting, but in the event of an equality of votes, the chairman shall have an additional casting vote. 45

(4) The quorum for a meeting of the Professional Conduct
Committee shall be five members of whom at least three shall be members of the General Council.

(5) A person who has been a member of the Investigating Committee or a sub-committee of that Committee during any part of the investigation by that Committee of any case shall not perform any function as a member of the Professional Conduct Committee in connection with the hearing of that case.

(6) Except in so far as provision is made by rules under section 16 or by this paragraph, the Professional Conduct Committee may regulate their own procedure.

The Health Committee

16.—(1) The Health Committee shall consist of—

(a) not less than six members appointed by the General Council from among its members, of whom at least two shall be such members as are referred to in paragraph 1(3) and, if practicable, one shall be a registered medical practitioner; and

(b) not more than four such other persons as may from time to time be members by virtue of paragraph 17.

(2) At any meeting of the Health Committee if the Chairman of the General Council is present he shall be Chairman and otherwise such member of the Committee as the Committee shall choose shall be chairman.

(3) All acts of the Health Committee shall be decided by a majority of the members present and voting, but in the event of an equality of votes, the chairman shall have an additional casting vote.

(4) The quorum for a meeting of the Health Committee shall be five members of whom at least three shall be members of the General Council.

(5) The Health Committee may appoint a sub-committee to perform any of their functions.

(6) A person who has been a member of the Investigating Committee or a sub-committee of that Committee during any part of the investigation by that Committee of any case shall not perform any function as a member of the Health Committee or any sub-committee of that Committee in connection with the hearing of that case.

(7) No decision of the Health Committee shall be invalidated by the absence of a member who is a registered medical practitioner.

(8) Except in so far as provision is made by rules under section 16 or by this paragraph, the Health Committee may regulate their own procedure.

Co-option of further members on to the Committees

17.—(1) Each of the Committees mentioned in this Part of this Schedule may, with the approval of the General Council, co-opt on to the Committee not more than four or, in the case of the Investigating Committee, eight further members at any time. 5

(2) In the case of the Education Committee those further members must be persons employed in teaching at an osteopathic training school or institution (other than a school or institution at which a member of the General Council such as is referred to in paragraph 1(4) is for the time being employed), and the General Council may 10 impose such restrictions on the categories of persons who may be co-opted on to the other Committees as they may think appropriate.

(3) A person who is a member of one of those Committees by virtue of sub-paragraph (1) shall not remain as such a member for a period exceeding three years. 15